To Lily Ella

enjoy the read!

Maria Whatton

X

HOMETOWN TALES
BIRMINGHAM

HOMETOWN TALES is a series of books pairing exciting new voices with some of the most talented and important authors at work today. Each of the writers has contributed an original tale on the theme of hometown, exploring places and communities in the UK where they have lived or think of as home.

Some of the tales are fiction and some are narrative non-fiction — they are all powerful, fascinating and moving, and aim to celebrate regional diversity and explore the meaning of home.

HOMETOWN TALES
BIRMINGHAM

MARIA WHATTON
STEWART LEE

WEIDENFELD & NICOLSON

First published in Great Britain in 2018 by Weidenfeld & Nicolson
an imprint of The Orion Publishing Group Ltd
Carmelite House, 50 Victoria Embankment
London EC4Y 0DZ

An Hachette UK Company

1 3 5 7 9 10 8 6 4 2

Silver in the Quarter © Maria Whatton 2018
In the Ape's Shadow © Stewart Lee 2018

The moral right of Maria Whatton and Stewart Lee to be identified
as the authors of this work has been asserted in accordance
with the Copyright, Designs and Patents Act of 1988.

Grateful acknowledgement is made to Steel Pulse for permission to quote
from 'Handsworth Revolution', to the Estate of Nikki Sudden for permission
to quote from 'Green Shield Stamps' and to Robert Lloyd for permission to
quote from 'Use Your Loaf' by The Nightingales.

A Boy Named Epic
Words and Music by David Graney
Copyright © 2003 Mushroom Music Pty Ltd.
All rights Administered by BGM Rights Management (US) LLC
All Rights Reserved Used by Permission
Reprinted by Permission of Hal Leonard LLC

All rights reserved. No part of this publication may be reproduced, stored in
a retrieval system, or transmitted in any form or by any means, electronic,
mechanical, photocopying, recording, or otherwise, without the prior
permission of both the copyright owner and the above publisher of this book.

Certain names and identifying characteristics have, on occasion,
been changed to protect the privacy of individuals.

A CIP catalogue record for this book is available from the British Library.

ISBN (Hardback) 978 1 4746 0594 6
ISBN (eBook) 978 1 4746 0595 3

Typeset at The Spartan Press Ltd, Lymington, Hants

Printed and bound in Great Britain by Clays Ltd, St Ives plc

www.orionbooks.co.uk

CONTENTS

Silver in the Quarter
Maria Whatton   1

In the Ape's Shadow
Stewart Lee   77

Silver in the Quarter

Maria Whatton

MARIA WHATTON was born in Liverpool and moved to the Midlands in the 1990s where she married a Birmingham firefighter and raised a family. She is a multi-award-winning storyteller who tours nationally and internationally telling ancient legends and folk tales. She lectures and performs in theatres, festivals and educational establishments.

To dearest David and my darling Maya

IT IS NOT often I think of it. A small silver locket. Sometimes if I'm in the barber's and a lump of hair falls to the floor, or if I smell the sharp vinegary tang of borax. Crafted shrapnel from the front line of childhood. An inheritance that I gave away so readily.

Dad was a jeweller, when he was well enough to work, and we lived in a clapped-out terraced house in Erdington, about five miles from the centre of Birmingham. Our house was our castle and as cold as old stone. Over the years, my father turned it into a fortress. The neighbours referred to my father as 'the Mad Dad'. There was no such thing as political correctness in Erdington in the 1970s. Dad was oblivious to his title. He was too busy dodging invisible bullets from snipers on rooftops as he walked down the road, or building a turbo-engined boat in the shed at the bottom of the garden. Only Dad could think of making an escape craft that would move on water, in the most landlocked part of the country.

Despite what we would nowadays refer to as mental health issues, but for which back then there were few kind words, Dad was a skilled craftsman. He had a workshop in the Jewellery Quarter in Birmingham, from where he would produce exquisite bracelets and finely wrought necklaces. His specialism was silver lockets. Little elegant cases, no bigger than a thumbnail, etched with elaborate patterns and as pretty as seashells. A locket was the perfect gift for a young lady's eighteenth birthday or an anniversary present from a husband to a wife. The locket's recipient would have the satisfaction of snapping shut the case to hide a lock of hair or an image of a loved one, and wearing a secret in plain sight. Dad's skill was much in demand. Back then, Christmas started in winter, unlike today when cards and decorations are in the shops by the back end of summer. That meant that when I was a kid, Dad had to produce thousands of those lockets and November was the month when it all began.

*

Silver in the Quarter

I was thirteen years old and had survived the first year at secondary school and was now halfway through my first term of second year at Witton Common. I'd passed the eleven-plus exam, but Mom said we couldn't afford that posh uniform, so I went to the local comp instead. I was glad. I was no snob. The girls had shorter skirts at the comp too, so that was good enough for me. I'd managed not to get my head put down the toilet like everyone had promised and even made a couple of friends, Lincoln and Derek.

It was Saturday morning. Early. I was fast asleep between purple nylon sheets Mom had got from the catalogue and was still paying for. The orange flowers on the curtains smiled in bright patterns as I opened my eyes.

'Oy, sleepin' ugly. Up. Yow comin' with me!'

Dad poked his head through the bedroom door. He had his hat on. He always had his hat on. It was a trilby that may as well have been a helmet. He had bought it from a gentleman's outfitters at a price that could have afforded us a day trip to Barmouth. It was during one of his 'episodes', when he claimed we were all out to get him. He hadn't taken it off since.

If Dad ordered you to do something, you did it. There was no point arguing. If you back chatted him, you'd get banjoed. I pulled on a T-shirt and jeans and thudded down the stairs, shovelling crunchy cornflakes into my mouth in seconds. At the bus stop, my tongue was still discovering delicious wedges of chobbled flakes between my unbrushed teeth. As the big blue and cream bus screeched to a stop next to us, I was completing my morning ablutions by scooping the sleep from the corner of my eyes with my little fingernail. It gave the same satisfaction as picking a scab.

It was only when we were halfway through the journey on the number 64 bus, I dared ask the question, 'Where are we going, Dad?' I guessed we would be out most of the day. The clue was inside Dad's bulging oilcloth bag that hung over his shoulder. I could see the white plastic cup handle of the flask poking out from the flap. There would be good, strong, tan-coloured tea in there, sweetened with heaps of white sugar. I was sure there would be thick corned beef sandwiches splashed with red sauce too. It made me feel hungry. My tongue poked around my teeth to see if I could uncover any more scraps of stuck breakfast cereal. It was still only 8.30 in the morning.

'Today, son, we are going to be Father Christmas's

elves and make presents for everyone who's been good,' he said. Then he swivelled his trilbied head towards the window and fell silent. I didn't know what he was going on about but knew that whatever it was, it was best to go along with it. Dad's mood could be brittle. If I'd boiled all the eggs from the eggshells I'd had to walk on, I could have made breakfast for Britain.

I longed for Dad to be a lullaby. He was more a boxing ring bell.

The bus stopped next to a big building, and without saying anything, Dad jumped up from his seat. I shot up after him. In those days there was no hush and hiss of a bus door opening to give you time to alight. There was an open space and it was the thing to leap off as the bus glided to a halt. It made you feel athletic, the air lamping you in the face.

The building in front of us looked very sure of itself. It was wearing a rectangular badge which said: Birmingham Post and Mail. I wondered if this was where we were going. I had no idea it was the place where newspapers were printed. It crossed my mind that Dad might believe Father Christmas really existed and had decided we would spend the day delivering letters for him.

The building loomed over us, looking like a giant had been given Lego bricks and then propped them up on sticks. It made me feel like I'd just arrived in the future. My eyes were on stalks. The cold sky shimmered across the big panes of glass and I twisted around behind Dad so I could look back at it.

Dad was clearly not stopping here. He was off. I chased after him, taking one more turn to look back.

We hardly ever came into town. I'd been twice with Mom when I was in junior school. We'd got straight off the bus which pulled up right outside Rackhams, wandered around the store so she could stare at all the things she couldn't afford, and then gone straight back home on the bus again. So on this trip with Dad everything was new to me. I wanted to burn everything I saw into my memory. I felt a tingle of excitement in the icy air as if something startling and fantastic was about to happen. I did consider the idea that Dad was going to head towards some boozer and I'd have to stand outside for ages in the cold, but I knew that was unlikely. It was too early in the day, even for Dad. I just kept walking fast, the unironed flares of my jeans flapping, slapping my shins as I tried to keep up with him.

We swerved down into an underpass and as we emerged from a dark tunnel I saw in front of me a mass of colour, curved round the wall. It was a picture of a man with hair that shone like spilled cough tonic. His smile made him look clever. The man was in the centre of the picture and there were crowds of people gazing up at him, trying to touch him, like he was God. As we got closer I saw that the picture was made up of thousands of little tiles all different colours.

'What's that?' I said, not necessarily expecting a reply. Dad would often take comfort in ignoring you. He was not a man of many words, well not unless he'd been drinking. Then he could rant for England. Today he was sober and Mom said he'd been taking his medication recently. So he was OK. There was always an edge to him, but he was usually fairly straightforward when he was on meds and had work. Today, as it happened, he was choosing to be conversive.

'Mosaic, son.' Dad replied.

Mo Zayic? I thought. I was confused. There was a woman down our road called Mo. Her real name was Maureen. Behind her back everyone called her Omo because she never stopped going on about having a fancy new washing machine. Many of the families by ours still had twin tubs. Omo was a washing powder everyone used back in the day. Mo was definitely a woman's name.

'Who is she then?'

'She?' said Dad, 'yow blind? It's John F. Kennedy, son. President of the United States of America. Got shot in the 'ead a few years back.'

I had never heard of him. I had also never seen art like that. My mind buzzed at the thought of some poor chap gluing on each individual tile, shivering his tits off in this cold, exposed street with traffic rushing past. I was in awe. It must have taken him ages. I had no idea why the dead president of the USA was here in the middle of Birmingham and I wasn't going to ask. It made me think of Derek, my mate at school. He was really good at art. He could draw anything. He'd even drawn a picture of Mr Potts, our form teacher, his baldy head and wonky glasses and everything. It was cock on.

I noticed there was writing down the sides of the Mo Zayik. Dad was walking so fast, I only caught the words 'yards of battle'. We were out of there, passing the Canning factory and onto Warstone Lane. It was full of grimy old buildings, with big arched windows. Hundreds of them, all with metal-framed rectangles inside them. They reminded me of the picture on the front of a copy of *David Copperfield* we were reading at school. There was a fancy clock in the middle of the road. It was almost 9 a.m. We walked past a building with more arched windows. It looked like a church, but the waft of beer near the doorway assured me it was a boozer.

We went a bit further down the street before Dad came abruptly to a standstill. He pushed open a chipped green door and at once the smell hit me. It was a mixture of disinfectant, burning magnesium ribbon, and iron filings. I was suddenly back at school, in my first ever chemistry lesson. Unlike our modern comprehensive Science Lab, this building was old. It had bright, whitewashed walls and a steep staircase leading to an unknown future.

I had no idea where we were. It seemed like there were hundreds of rooms in this building and each closed door muffled the sound of tapping, banging and mumbled voices. I knew there was no such thing as Father Christmas, but I secretly desired that we would reach a room where we'd be met by a big jolly-faced man with happy blue eyes and a white beard, wearing a red tunic.

Dad opened a door. There were two men wearing big oily overalls and I could see immediately that they were not elves. They were two blokes called Eric and Sandeep. Dad didn't introduce them to me, they introduced themselves. Dad ignored them and went straight to a workbench. He took off his coat, but the hat stayed firmly on his head. Dad started getting tools out of a drawer and laying them on the bench in front of him.

'Yow Peter's lad then?' said Sandeep, nodding towards Dad's back. Sandeep was holding what looked like a bangle in one hand and a heavy metal file in the other. It was the size and shape of a Toblerone.

I nodded.

'I'm Sandeep,' he said, 'and this 'ere is Eric.'

Eric was sitting by his bench, hammering away at something flat and metallic with real intensity. Eric continued to tap rhythmically, not taking his eyes off his work. 'All right, son,' he said cheerfully, his eyes glued to the wafer of metal on the bench. Eric spoke without removing the cigarette stuck to his bottom lip. 'Wha's ya name, son?'

'Luke,' I said.

This was at a time when I was publicly still called by my first name. At school my mates now referred to me as Warmsy (as in, luke warm). Three years later everyone would be calling me Skywalker, which then got abbreviated to Walker and then Walksy. So I went from Warmsy to Walksy, from boy to man. They were fond of a good nickname at Witton Common.

'Yow 'ere to 'elp yer dad, Luke?' Sandeep was a small, sturdy man with a face that looked as open as the first page of a new book.

I had no idea, so I couldn't answer. I grinned and shrugged my shoulders.

'Well don't be shy,' he said, 'we know Pete 'ere is very... quiet, but me and Eric, we ain't.'

With that, he reached across the bench towards a little transistor radio. He turned up the crackling sound. It was Matt Munro singing 'I Will Wait For You'.

Immediately, Sandeep and Eric began to warble along. I marvelled at how Eric managed to sing and never remove the cigarette from his mouth.

Sandeep returned to his bench. A twist of smoke from Eric's cigarette followed Sandeep through the air like a loyal puppy.

*

That afternoon, Dad taught me how to piece together those lockets. Screwing in the tiny hinges and filing the edges. He showed me how to use the large machine press that banged the metal with a flourish. There was a weight the size of a small planet on it that helped it hammer down with the ferocity of an anvil, bludgeoning the metal into a steely flat square. I filed rough metal until it was smooth and as shiny as glass. The dust filled the air and danced inside the smoke exhaled by Dad, Sandeep and Eric's cigarettes.

Dad was an alchemist, filing a powder from a cone of pale borax and making a paste with clear alcohol, that looked as innocent as water. We painted the paste onto the joints of lockets so that when we soldered them they did not turn black. Dad was a magician firing a blowtorch and I was the magician's apprentice. We didn't wear gloves or protective glasses or face masks. It was 1974 and Engelbert Humperdinck was on the radio singing 'please release me, let me go' and Sandeep and Eric were yodelling along, enraptured. Dad, who hadn't once acknowledged their presence mumbled, 'Daft sods.'

The white light that had entered crisply through the large windows in the morning dimmed by the

Silver in the Quarter

afternoon. Hooded electric lamps were switched on, adding a yellow haze to the cigarette smoke and filed particles hovering in the air. Sandeep and Eric were still humming tunes, but when I looked across at them they were like ghosts in a boat on a foggy lake, moving through mist but still anchored to us by their strangled melodies.

By five o'clock it was dark. Sandeep and Eric emerged from the haze, hung up their aprons and replaced them with donkey jackets. 'See ya, kid,' they said, 'and yow, Pete.' Dad ignored them. I gave a wave and hoped Dad wouldn't think I was a traitor. I was sure Sandeep and Eric were OK, even though Dad obviously had no time for them. You could say the most ordinary thing to Dad sometimes and he'd think you were having a pop at him.

I thought that Dad and I would leave the workshop then too, but Dad carried on going. By now my fingers were aching from filing and polishing. I was hungry too. I'd been right about the corned beef and tomato sauce sandwiches. They had been bostin', but my stomach was telling me that it needed to be filled again. I kept expecting him to down tools and take off his apron. He carried on.

*

It was six thirty when Dad finally started to lay out all the lockets and count them. He spread out a scroll of soft cloth and placed each locket side by side onto it. They formed a shimmering undulation that covered the width and length of two benches. It was a mermaid's tail of treasure. Under the lamplight, I saw we had created something to be proud of. I was very chuffed with myself. I hoped Dad was going to thank me or say well done, but he was more like Fagin, the brim of his trilby casting a shadow over his face as he counted then recounted.

Dad put the scroll of cloth in a locked drawer. Then he packed a separate smaller roll into his bag and passed me the thermos flask. He could no longer fit it in his bag. Meticulously he put away his tools, and just before he turned out all the lamps, I noticed the piles of silvery dust that had settled in the corners of the room. It glittered on the shelves and the floor and the window ledges. For a moment it felt like we had been in Santa's workshop after all.

The cold bit into my fingers and face out on the dark lane. I hugged the thermos against my duffel coat. The Victorian street lights shed pools of yellow light into the shadowy pavement. I had a good idea which

Silver in the Quarter

way we needed to go to get back to the bus stop. I'd taken note of every twist and turn, building and street sign on the way, so when Dad began to cross in the wrong direction, I presumed he knew an alternative way home.

'Wait 'ere!' he said as we reached the bulky trunk of the ornate clock. 'I ain't gonna be long.'

''Ere?'

The clock was in the middle of a traffic island. I suddenly felt like Robinson Crusoe.

Dad's face looked pinched. His eyes were shadows under the rim of his trilby. His mouth was thin. His teeth looked grey.

'I said I wo' be long,' he repeated.

I watched as he trotted across the road and disappeared in to the church I'd seen earlier that morning that had stunk of booze.

I stamped my feet against the ground and tried to keep warm. There were hardly any people about. Every now and then a man appeared out of the darkness and was visible for the seconds he was caught in the light of the street lamp. Inevitably these men would slink into the pub where Dad was now drinking. I tried to camouflage myself by putting my hood up and leaning into the shin of the clock.

After forty-five minutes, Dad appeared, shoving two bags of crisps at me and a bottle of pop. Then he vanished again. I had to place the thermos on the floor so I could manage my al fresco dining arrangements. I ripped the crisp bags open ferociously. I gorged on them, crunching crazily, then swilling them down with the fizz from the glass bottle. The pop was ice-cold and intensely sweet. I'd polished the lot off in minutes, even tipping my head back and pouring the crumbs from the crisp packets into my mouth so that I could get every last salt speck onto my tongue.

There were no mobile phones in those days. We did have a phone at home, a big clunky thing with a circular dial for each number. However, we did not have our own line. We had what was called a party line and we shared it with the family across the road. They were always talking to their relatives, so we hardly ever got a chance to use it. If you really wanted to, you could pick up the phone and earwig on their conversations, night or day. I was not interested in the slightest about hearing how Ethel had gone very thin, or Jack had been taken into a home. I did, however, sometimes notice Mom benignly stuck to the earpiece, having a good old snoop.

Silver in the Quarter

*

If you were away from home, the only way to make a phone call would be to use a telephone box, but I had no two-pence pieces with me. Dad had all the money. Also, by now, Mom would be serving behind the bar of The Hare and Hounds, where she was a barmaid. The neighbours we shared the line with would be gassing away to Minnie or Myrtle about something and nothing, and I'd never get through anyway.

I entertained myself by identifying each car that curved around the edge of the island I'd been stranded on. Bored, cold and restless, I became braver, running the gauntlet of the traffic to memorise the string of parked cars further up the lane and off the side roads. After each outing I would return to the barrel of the clock and assemble the list in my head like a poem:

> Triumph Herald, Ford Cortina,
> Hillman Hunter, Morris Marina,
> Austin Maxi, Ford Capri,
> Morris Mini, Sports MG.

I wanted to find a yellow Ford Escort Mexico, not for its rhyming potential, but because it was my dream car. I hoped to find one so I could imagine myself as an adult sitting behind the wheel, a rev of the engine away from freedom. I scanned the roads. No luck. I trudged back to the clock. I stamped my feet and pleaded with a God I did not believe in to get him to return Dad back to me sober.

God didn't listen. Dad, a blur of shadow with a swag bag, staggered towards me. The clock face stared down at him like a headmistress standing at the school gates. It was six minutes past ten.

Dad made no excuses. He said exactly nothing. He pushed a pile of coins into my fist and began to walk away from me. A couple of coins tinkled to the ground and into the darkness. I could not see where they'd gone. I had no time to try and find them. Dad was zigzagging away, ahead of me. Of course I followed. The bag was still in place on his shoulder. It looked as stuffed full as it had been hours ago. I felt relieved. I couldn't bear the thought of all those lockets we'd spent hours making being stolen.

Somehow we made it to the bus stop. When the bus came, I had to push Dad up the aisle and onto a seat, where he promptly pressed his shoulder against the window and fell asleep. His head tipped forward. His hat stayed put. The worst part was trying to get him to move when it came to our stop. He would not wake up. The bus shuddered on the spot. One person got on, but we were too late to get off. Now we would have to walk home even further.

To add to the misery, when we did get off at the next stop, it was raining. Yes, God definitely hadn't been listening. I pulled Dad's arm around my shoulder and propped him up as we walked. Rain trickled from the brim of his trilby and found a secret tunnel down to my bare neck. Every time I tried to walk forward in a straight line, Dad pushed me towards the kerb or alternatively towards the prickly privet hedges which skirted the front gardens. Every so often I would have to stop, give him a shove, then begin again.

We had just got to Osborne Road when I saw two figures coming towards me. It was definitely two blokes. I could hear the lower tones of their laughter and chat. One was taller than the other. They had their collars up. They were wearing denim jackets and flared trousers. My heart sank. I prayed they weren't thieves. Dad was carrying a bag full of riches that meant this year we'd have Christmas dinner and presents. There was no way they were getting that bag.

I was still fighting with Dad to keep him upright. They were getting closer. I looked towards them, ready to stare them down with my most fierce glare. *Don't say a word*, I thought, *don't even think of trying to take Dad's bag*. I tried to set my teenage face into a cocked gun, a drawn sword, a pointed dagger, but when they got within a few feet of me, I saw that the smaller figure was none other than my mate Lincoln from school. We made eye contact as we passed. Neither of us said a word. Lincoln's eyes inflated with shock. It was momentary, but I could see he was horrified. He didn't say anything. They passed.

Shame began to seep into me like rain into dry earth. Now what would happen when I saw Lincoln in school on Monday? He'd either make fun of me, tell everyone my dad was a wasted old piss head, or avoid me. I didn't know which was worse. Dad was heavier than ever and I hated him. His breath puffed out of him in little clouds of pickled onion and beer. There were still two more long roads before I got home. I wanted to shake him off my shoulder, dump him on the wet ground and leave him there. There was a shout inside me so loud that I had to grit my teeth together to stop it bursting out. My eyes were getting hot. I tried to suppress a tear that trembled in the corner of my eye.

Then suddenly Dad lost weight. One second he was as heavy as an elephant, the next as light as a feather. Dad was still attached to me. His arm was still tangled round my neck, but his body became less of a burden. Someone else was lifting Dad up on his right-hand side. It happened very quickly. It was the taller bloke that had been walking with Lincoln. I stared across and saw that this taller bloke looked a lot like Lincoln. His hair was bigger, his face was more angular, but his eyes were definitely the same. When he spoke, he sounded different to Lincoln. He had a much stronger Jamaican accent.

'Linc ses you and 'im are mates. Dat right?'

'Yes,' I squeaked.

'Dis your fatha?' He looked towards the trilby.

'Yes.'

'No problem. Some fathas like dat.'

We were now walking together like this was normal. Normal having a drunken old sod, paralytic with drink, being carried home by his thirteen-year-old son and a stranger.

Next thing, Lincoln is walking along the other side

of me, head down and hands in pockets. 'This is me brother Dewain,' said Lincoln in explanation, while staring at his feet. 'He says we have to 'elp you get your dad 'ome.'

And they did. Not only did Dewain carry most of the burden of Dad for those last two streets, but he also frisked him like a copper to find his house keys when we got to our front door. Dewain put Dad on the settee and propped him up with cushions. Thankfully he heeded my request not to touch his hat when he went to helpfully remove it.

*

The next day was taken up with Dad accusing me of being a bloody idiot. He had completely eradicated the memory of me helping him make all that jewellery and leaving me on my own with only a Victorian clock for company, in the freezing cold, while he got kaylied. He conveniently remembered, however, that the thermos flask was missing and that he had told me to look after it.

As much as I wanted to shout back at him that I'd had more pressing demands, like looking after a drunken old sod, who could barely walk, I didn't.

Silver in the Quarter

This was six months before my growth spurt and I was still shorter than him and aware of how hard his fists could be.

Mom was no help as usual. She said she had a gigantic headache and she kept putting her hands against her head, circling the heel of her palms against her temples. This only seemed to wind Dad up more.

I had looked at the clock on my bedside table when I heard her put the key in the lock. It was 2.30 a.m. I could never properly sleep until she returned. I thought it was terrible the way Bob at the pub made her work until such a late hour. There must have been hundreds and hundreds of glasses to wash up after everybody left. In those days pubs closed at 10.30 p.m.

Dad was not appeased until Mom pointed to a picture of a similar-looking thermos flask in the catalogue which was only 20p a week for six weeks. She was already filling in the form.

'Well 'e can contribute to tha' with 'is pockit munny,' said Dad, pointing at me. 'Yow 'ave to learn a lesson 'bout takin' responsibilitay!'

With that, Dad picked up the oilcloth bag, that I'd

helped to keep on his shoulder the night before, and went out the house.

The peace that resided in the absence of Dad's presence was always the most enjoyable. It was like a weight had lifted and the house became a place to relax, even if you knew it was only temporary and that the returned Dad may be much worse than the one who'd just left. That would be something to worry about later. For now, Mom could get her knitting out, push her glasses up her face and curl her toes under her knees on the settee. There'd be a paper bag of sherbet lemons crinkled open next to her feet that you could help yourself to.

I had no need to be concerned about Dad's return home that night or what Lincoln might say the next day. As it turned out, Dad had bumped into Mavis and Harry who ran the local Communist Party, on his way out that afternoon. They seemed to be the only people round by ours who would a) spend any time with Dad, and b) be able to dissuade him from going to the pub by offering him gallons of tea and an ear on his opinions. Dad loved to wax lyrical about the Tories forcing us to join the European Union last year and the problems we now had with a minority Labour government. Obviously Mavis and Harry had their own agenda, but I loved them for it. Consequently, Dad returned home that Sunday evening, sober and with plenty of *Morning Star* newspapers to keep him occupied.

*

In school on the Monday, Lincoln never said a word about Saturday night. We'd played footy on the field and Derek had scored three goals between our blazers. We had a right laugh on Tuesday lunchtime with some girls from the year above and Derek had offered Karen Dalby one of his cheese triangles, as though he was the man from the Milk Tray advert, opening the round lid and speaking to her in a fake Scottish accent like he was Sean Connery. The girls had laughed until I thought Lisa Hagan was going to wet herself. There is nothing more intoxicating for a thirteen-year-old boy than hearing girls laugh wholeheartedly at your jokes. That lunchtime we were on fire.

Lisa Hagan had a smile like a *Jackie* magazine cover girl and her hair was a sweep of magnificent bronze and gold. Mom got a fancy box of biscuits every year for Christmas and I had never forgotten the picture on the lid of one of them. It was a painting of a beautiful girl in a boat that looked like it was straight out of a King Arthur tale. On the back of the box was the title 'The Lady of Shalott'. The girl in the boat was the spitting image of Lisa Hagan, pale, elegant and with tresses of red hair flowing down over her shoulders. Lisa made me wish I looked like David Essex or David Cassidy, when I knew I bore more of a resemblance to Noddy Holder, just missing the sideburns.

*

On Wednesday Mr Arrowsmith the music teacher told us that we were allowed to use the music room at lunchtimes if we were going to learn an instrument, and that included guitars. He also said that if me, Lincoln and Derek could sing, we could join the choir. Bullseye. We didn't give a monkey's what anyone else said, Karen Dalby and Lisa Hagan, along with a host of other gorgeous girls, were in the choir. This would involve a trip into Birmingham in a few weeks' time, but we'd get to perform at the Town Hall. We three nodded. In our own heads we were already at the beginning of our careers as rock gods. I was on a

Silver in the Quarter

high. Could this week get any better? Well yes, was the answer. On Thursday afternoon as we sauntered out of the school gates, Lincoln turned to me and said, 'Wanna come back to ours Warmsy?'

The Millers lived in a terraced house about a mile away from us. It struck me immediately what the main difference was between my house and Lincoln's. The order. This was a well-maintained home. It looked explosively colourful and simultaneously rigorously neat. Our house was always untidy. There were always plates and cups on the coffee table in our living room, alongside a ragged heap of newspapers, ripped open letters and magazines. Coats would be dumped on the backs of chairs and remain there like hunched men waiting at the bookies.

Not here. The living room was small with a green vinyl settee. Eight equidistant buttons decorated the back of it. I could see there were no crumbs inhabiting the ridges or creases. There were two other chairs with splayed wooden legs that had been made cosy by two crocheted mantles that were vibrant orange, green and yellow. The floor was immaculate. The sideboard and stereo player were spotless and the room smelt of furniture polish and spice. There was a sunray clock on the wall and a colourful painting of floppy roses.

Lincoln ran upstairs and returned in minutes fully changed. He was now in his casual gear, flared jeans and a yellow T-shirt. I would realise very soon why he was so quick to hang up his uniform neatly and present himself in the living room changed and ready to help. The reason entered the house carrying two string bags full of shopping. Lincoln had clearly been trained well. The bags were out of her hands and on the kitchen table. Everything was being put away with an efficiency that I had not experienced in our house. This was Lincoln's mother, Mrs Rosi Miller.

Her immediate presence was purposeful and powerful. She was a substantial woman, dressed in royal blue. Her coat matched her dress in fabric and style. She had bright orange lipstick and wore pearls around her neck. She had been shopping, but I was to learn that Mrs Miller's appearance was very important to her even while she was performing the most perfunctory task. I once saw her scrubbing the front path to that house wearing a pink and gold dress and a soft scarlet hat pinned to her head. She held her head high so you never really noticed that she was undertaking a menial job. Everybody knew Mrs Miller. Mrs

Miller knew everybody. She was distinguished in her unceasing refinement.

Finally, when all the shopping was cleared away, she turned to me.

'Ah,' she said, 'yuh Lincoln's friend?' Her accent was identical to Dewain's.

I nodded and felt like I had shrunk to the size of an infant.

'Dewain tell mi all bout yuh fatha.'

My heart jumped. Lincoln and I had happily not referred to this incident in five days. Now here was Mrs Miller talking about it openly as though it were common knowledge. I had only just met her. She was breaking all the rules. She sat down on the green vinyl settee and I could hear the exhalation of the cushion's breath as she settled herself.

'Mi tell Lincoln to invite yuh,' she said, 'now listen. Mi see you 'ave problem with yuh fatha, but one-eye man a king in blindman country.'

She smiled. I didn't have the faintest clue what she was talking about. She stared at me with such a fierce kindness that although I was reeling with shock from her honesty, I was also peculiarly reassured that she had an eye on me, in a good way.

'Listen,' she continued, 'sum fathas just like dat.'

She shrugged her shoulders and I heard Dewain's words repeated. For the first time ever I felt like someone was accepting that life could be a little bit shit but you could get through it. Here was someone who knew that I had a Mad Dad and yet didn't look down on me.

Mrs Miller allowed Lincoln and I to go up to his bedroom while she cooked dinner. It was a room that he shared with Dewain.

'Dewain won't be back from work for ages, he's on lates,' said Lincoln, 'so while 'e's not here we can listen to these.'

He pointed to a black plastic box next to Dewain's bed. He knelt down and opened the lid. I noted a measure of caution in his handling as he slipped out three bright splashes of record sleeves and lay them on the floor. There was an old Dansette record player in the corner. Lincoln asked me to choose one of the three records and spread them on the floor like a hand of cards. I wasn't familiar with any of them, so I plumped for the one in the middle. 'Good choice,' said Lincoln beaming, as he lowered the hole in the centre of the LP onto the spindle. I had chosen Bob

Silver in the Quarter

Marley and the Wailing Wailers, three young men in dapper suits and very shiny shoes.

This was the first time I ever heard reggae music. My heart reacted like Lincoln's torso. Still kneeling over the deck, he was swaying to the rhythm, his arms gently lapping the air like he was about to fly. His eyes were closed and he was unselfconsciously singing along. Together, our heads bobbed at exactly the same time. The music was a magic wand forcing us to move whether we wanted to or not. I had always thought dancing was ridiculous, now I couldn't help myself. Both of us got up and moved to the compulsive beats.

'Careful, man,' said Lincoln when I started to get a bit too enthusiastic, 'Dewain'll kill me if any of these get scratched.'

We managed to groove around without hurting Dewain's precious collection. Dewain had helped me out with Dad and I felt grateful for that. He was also nineteen and a lot bigger than me and I did not want to get on the wrong side of him.

That night I was introduced to jerk chicken, rice and peas – although they weren't the kind of peas that I was familiar with. The peas I knew came out of a packet from the freezer, and were green; these were brown and a little bit slimy. It was the chicken that caught my throat. I had only ever been used to the blandest of food: wet cabbage, mashed potato, sausages, that kind of thing. I had never eaten a curry, except one that Mom had bought from the Co-op in a packet called 'Vesta Curry'. That hadn't tasted of anything much at all. I imagined it was what wallpaper paste tasted like if wallpaper paste were brown.

We were sitting around the table eating. Mrs Miller was at the top, and Lincoln's two little sisters Oria and Steebeth next to us. Mr Miller was 'away' and Dewain on a 'late'. When I started to choke on the spicy food, both the little girls giggled with uncontrollable glee. Mrs Miller, however, was an agile restorer of composure. One cough plus a harsh stare returned the girls to eating their dinners quietly. A guest was not going to be disrespected at her table. Lincoln was sent to fetch cold water from the tap. My dad referred to that as council pop. I glugged it down. I kept trying to apologise, but each time I attempted it my throat hissed and my face became red again. Mrs Miller was gracious about it, but I could tell she was slightly miffed that I hadn't been in heaven over her food. She rated herself a damn fine cook. In fact, over time it was Mrs Miller who would introduce me to a whole new cuisine: fried plantain, ackee and salt fish and callaloo greens, curried goat, patties and dumplings. I don't know how it happened, but I grew to love that food. Even today when I eat Jamaican food it tastes of sanctuary and solace.

I returned from the sanity of the Millers to find Dad rummaging in drawers. Cupboards were being probed, investigated, their contents dispatched. There was a bolt lock resting on the kitchen table next to a hand drill. The sound of Dad searching always put me on edge. Another father with a hammer and nails might indicate a bit of light DIY. With Dad it signalled something much bigger. It was like the time he'd decided to make the boat. That was still half finished and wedged awkwardly into the shed in the garden. He had been convinced that we'd all need it in case of a flood. Of course the flood never came, just some general Birmingham drizzle, easily dealt with by a standard umbrella. Dad put the boat-building on hold eventually, but only after months of obsessing about it to the point where he could no longer go to work. The boat took priority. That's when Mom took the job in The Hare and Hounds. We had bills to pay and food to be put on the table. Dad's projects were warning signs.

That night, Dad commandeered the front room for himself. He dragged the table from the kitchen and installed it in the centre of the front room. He screwed the bolt onto the inside of the door and locked himself in. He had made the settee into a makeshift bed. When Mom came home from work in the small hours of the morning, she found the front room door stuck fast. I woke to hear her hammering her fists against it and shouting for Dad to open up. Her pleas were met with curses. I could hear her begging him to take his medicine and him saying she was trying to poison him. When she went to bed, I could hear her gentle sobs in the bedroom next to mine.

It was coming to the end of November. Christmas would be poking its head round the door very soon, whether Dad was working or not. Mom might have to take on even more shifts at The Hare and Hounds to get us through. There'd been a record in the charts a few years ago by Dave Edmunds and, for some reason, every time I turned our little transistor on it was playing. It was like he was singing directly to me and Mom, 'I hear you knockin' but you can't come in.'

Silver in the Quarter

No matter what we said or did, Dad had barricaded himself into the living room and would only come out for something to eat or drink. I never mentioned it to Derek or Lincoln. When I was at school, I could forget about what Dad was up to.

I was by now besotted by Lisa Hagan and determined to learn guitar to impress her. I had passed the shorthand and typing classroom one day and spotted her through the window. There she was, the stream of shiny hair pushed neatly behind her ears, back straight, fingers hammering away at speed across the typewriter keys. I wanted to believe that in the future I could be her boss and she my secretary, and yet something in her poise and focus suggested that those roles would be better served reversed. There was an assuredness about her mastery over the machine that I craved to equal with my guitar.

Lincoln and I spent our lunchtimes either learning songs for the choir or trying to work out reggae rhythms on our school guitars while Derek knocked seven shades out of a set of drums. We annoyed each other so much, we should have been constantly at war, but with friendship, once you've found an oasis, you don't poison the nectar. Squabbles were always resolved. Derek's creative comedy helped. If there was ever a bit of tension between us, he would break it like he was snapping a KitKat in two. He'd suddenly be Eamonn Andrews with an authentic Irish accent that he'd stolen from his mom and dad who were from County Derry.

'Luke Warmsy Wilton, THIS IS YOUR LIFE! Dern, dern, deeeeern!'

He would then hand you any old book he could lay his hands on in the music room: *English Folk Ballads of the Seventeenth Century* or *Chopin – Genius Composer*, it didn't matter, he'd open it and it would transform into Eamonn's red book.

'There's a whole bunch of tossers here, Mr Luke Wilton, and they all can't wait to tell you what a fecker you are, but in the meantime can I introduce you to your old school friend. You knew him as a dowdy schoolkid, you haven't seen him for ten years, but now he is more famous than Jimi Hendrix... Welcome Lincoln Miller...'

Cue Lincoln jumping forward, guitar in hand, strumming a plectrum tunelessly across the strings like he was Elvis.

*

Silver in the Quarter

It was with great disappointment we learned that we had to wear our uniforms to the concert at the Town Hall. I spent ages getting ready at home, examining myself in the mirror. I fluffed up my hair, the back of which had grown long enough to touch the top edge of my shirt collar. I wet a comb and dragged it through my fringe in an attempt to create two small tunnels either side of my centre parting. I stole a squirt of Mom's hairspray to keep it in place. I pressed my school trousers so that there was a sharp crease down the front and made sure I scrubbed away an errant spot of red sauce from my school jumper.

Mr Arrowsmith had told us that we had to be there by 6.30 p.m. or we would get a detention. 'Punctuality is vital,' he said.

Mom could not make it because she was working in the pub that night and Dad was doing his hermit act in our front room. I was relieved he wouldn't be coming. I promised Mrs Miller that I would call for Lincoln and we'd get the bus together. She wanted to come but had Oria and Steebeth to look after. She took a step back when she saw us ready to leave.

'Look at yuh two. Yuh nuh look handsome.'

She leaned forward and picked out a tiny ball of

fluff lodged in Lincoln's hair. Lincoln knew best not to recoil from her mollycoddling. If he did, he'd feel the firm presence of Mrs Miller's palm.

'God, she's embarrassing,' he said as soon as we were out the door.
This was the first time I had ever been allowed to travel into town without an adult and I knew it was the same for Lincoln. It was a half-hour bus ride, but for us it was as adventurous as if we had been setting out on an expedition to Peru. It was the moment when growing up began. I was the experienced one, having been on my bus trip with Dad to the Jewellery Quarter. There had been a benefit to getting Dad home that night. My knowledge of the city centre was based on survival.

The Rotunda was a large cylinder that had grown out of a twisted shoebox in the centre of town. Light gleamed from horizontal bands of windows that ran up to the very top. There was a bracelet of advertising around its ankle shouting about Double Diamond and as we walked past it Lincoln and I started singing the tune from the advert 'Double Diamond works wonders...' at exactly the same time.

Silver in the Quarter

We laughed all the way up New Street, even more when an old tramp shouted 'Bloody darky' to Lincoln, to which I responded, 'Piss off wanker.' I had begun to learn the art of insult tennis. You did not allow a hurling ball of hurt whistling towards you past your racket. You made sure you hit back with the force of a champion. Swearing was fairly new to me, but I'd picked up some fine new expletives in my fifteen months at Witton Common.

When we reached the Town Hall there was already a queue of kids from our school. It was a bitter night and people were hugging their blazers. From a distance they looked like a line of heavy smokers as they exhaled warm puffs of air into the icy indigo night.

I spotted Lisa Hagan near the front and I tried to push in to get near her but got shoved back with a firm 'Piss off, Warmsy' from a dozen or so kids from the year above. She saw me though. She looked at me and smiled. For a moment I imagined myself older, suaver, pulling up next to her in a bright yellow Ford Escort Mexico, winding down the window, and saying, 'Wanna lift, bab?' It gave me a shiver of warm pleasure against the cold.

'D'yow see that, Linc?'

'Wha?'

Lincoln was distracted. He was turning his head, looking back into the distance of New Street.

'Lisa Hagan just looked at me.'

'So wha?' said Lincoln.

'Wha' yow lookin' for?'

'Derek. It's nearly half six. He ain't here yet.'

'Oh arr.'

It hadn't occurred to me.

The line was beginning to move. We were shuffling forward. Mr Arrowsmith was at the front.

'Come on, ladies and gents,' he was wearing a three-piece brown suit with a dickie bow tie, 'in you come now. Hope you're all in fine voice tonight. Get those tonsils at the ready.'

There was an empty seat as we sat on the stage. Derek had still not turned up.

'You can tell Mr O'Malley from me,' Mr Arrowsmith whispered, 'tomorrow he is in big trouble.'

'He might have missed the bus, sir,' Lincoln pleaded on Derek's behalf, but Mr Arrowsmith was off positioning himself in front of us all, striking his arms high above his head like he was about to grab an apple from an invisible tree.

Silver in the Quarter

*

The concert had been going for about an hour when I thought I heard a thud. I couldn't tell whether it was internal or external. Did that happen inside me? The girls' choir carried on singing 'Down by the Sally Gardens', a lyrical ballad that could easily set you off to sleep. I thought the girls' choir sounded a bit like angels, but very soon those celestial voices were being accompanied by distant fire bells. My ears strained to hear. They seemed to be growing closer. I looked out at the well-behaved audience that an hour ago had daunted me. There were a few people sitting at the back beginning to look at each other. A tiny thread of unease began to stitch its way silkily along the back rows.

As we sang our finale, the sound of the fire trucks was interloping timpani clashing against our harmonies.

It was only as we poured out of the Town Hall that we began to get a sense of what had happened. There was a stunned quiet into which a fearful thrum was beating in the distance. Inside the darkness an assailant had crept through Birmingham's ribcage and sliced through its heart. There was the smell of burning.

Rubber, salt, wood, chemicals. Smoke drifted upwards into a spray of shocked stars. More fire bells clanged. Blue lights blinked, while ambulances screamed a frenzy of urgency. The scene magnetised Lincoln and I towards it. We walked like zombies side by side, picking up our pace towards the bottom of New Street, now clogged with fire trucks and ambulances. We squeezed through the stationary traffic and into New Street Station. No one stopped us. On the other side there was the Rotunda building that we had past only hours ago. The lowest floor was completely devastated. Firemen in hard yellow helmets and brass-buttoned tunics were pulling at hoses, running into the shredded entrance.

We didn't utter a word. The smoke crawled towards us. A man clutching his wife limped past us. We could hear crying; someone was shouting. Someone was calling out, 'He's inside, he's still inside.' Somewhere a woman was sobbing, sobbing.

A fire truck was blocking the way, but we could make out that it was the pub at the foot of the Rotunda. All the windows had vanished. There were great gaping holes and gigantic splinters of debris poking out. I saw four firemen carrying what looked like a person on the back of a table to an ambulance.

Silver in the Quarter

The bright yellow helmets and trousers of the firemen clashed against the shocked shadows, like daffodils in a graveyard.

'Luke, Lincoln!' It was Mr Arrowsmith. He was sweating. His bow tie was skew-whiff. He looked like a man who had been running around, trying to herd cats.

'You need to get yourselves home lads.'

'What's 'appened, sir?'

'We don't know yet,' said Mr Arrowsmith, 'best get yourselves out of here.'

He turned us around and sent us in the opposite direction.

It was weird that night. It was like the whole of Birmingham was wondering around in panic and shock. We found a phone box and tried to phone Mom, but the neighbours were on the party line and we couldn't get through. Lincoln's family didn't have a phone. All the buses had stopped.

'It can't be that far to Erdington,' I said to Lincoln. We looked up and saw a road sign to Sutton Coldfield. 'Well, it's definitely in that direction, ai it?'

*

Someone at Mom's pub had been listening to the ten o'clock news on the radio and had come into The Hare and Hounds to tell the landlord what had happened. When Mom heard that there had been two bombings in Birmingham, she had clasped hold of the beer pumps to steady herself. Bob the landlord was immediately at her side. He put his arms around her to keep her upright and then poured her a whisky. She had taken one sip and run back home. Even though she'd hammered on the door to the living room and begged Dad to open it, he had refused. She had told him something had happened in Birmingham, something terrible, but that just made him more frightened. He told her to go away. She sat in the kitchen where there was now no longer a table and put her head in her hands. Then there was a knock on the front door.

*

All the way home Lincoln and I stopped to ask people directions. I was surprised that there were so many people around on a Thursday night in November. They were all helpful. Although some of them sent us the long way round, it was definitely through overzealous kindness not spite. On a night when unimaginable horror came to be a reality, other worse nightmares did not. Two schoolkids alone in the dark trying to find their way home were aided by total strangers.

The darkness became a blanket which wrapped around us as we walked, the rhythm of our feet the prosody of understanding. We started talking about our families. Lincoln told me how he, his mom, dad and Dewain had come to England when he was only seven. He said when they first arrived that they had lived with his Aunt Eralia in Handsworth.

'It was great there,' he said, 'but Dad wanted a proper home for us, so once he'd got a job at Hardy Spicer we moved to Erdington.'

I asked him if he could remember anything about Jamaica. He fell silent for a few seconds, then took a deep breath, 'Yeh, course I can' and before I knew it he was painting the landscape around us with his memories. As he spoke, the street lamps transformed into soaring palm trees, the cold pavement rose with heat and dust. The high-rise flats on the Lichfield Road became distant blue mountains, the swish of passing cars, the sound of the sea. I was in the middle of a marketplace where women wore dazzling turbans and aprons. I could smell the fresh sweet zest of fruits and pungent herbs mingling with filthy gutter water. I could hear the bony clack of tiles as Lincoln described his dad playing dominoes with his friends in the shade of the sultry heat. I watched those men huddled reverently around the board until one of them won and exploded wildly with joy.

'And it was always 'ot,' Lincoln said. 'Took me ages to get used to always 'aving to wear woolly jumpers 'ere.' Lincoln banished the vision of Jamaica with a shudder of cold. He had brought the land of his birth to the streets of Birmingham and I noted how the city of Birmingham had placed itself on his tongue. He had been such a little kid when he arrived in this country, it was inevitable he would acquire the local accent. That's why he sounded different to his mom and Dewain.

Lincoln confided in me that his dad was now back in Jamaica. Both his grandparents were ill and Lincoln's dad had made a difficult choice to return and support them. Dewain had got an apprenticeship at the same place his dad had been employed – Hardy Spicer. He was working shifts and had become the main breadwinner. He was keeping the family going. Lincoln told me he missed his dad. He asked me about

Silver in the Quarter

my dad. I explained that he was ill and that he was often a nightmare to live with. He asked me why my mom didn't leave him and I said, 'I think it's because we've got nowhere else to go.'

It was ten minutes before midnight when we found my front door in the darkness. The weirdest thing was the door was opened not by Mom or Dad but by Mrs Miller. She threw her arms round Lincoln and I thought he was going to die on the spot of suffocation. 'Mercy,' she muttered over and over as she braced him in her arms.

Mom was close behind her. 'Oh dear God,' she said with tears streaming down her face, 'I 'ad you dead and buried.'

We were ushered into the kitchen where Dewain was standing. He looked too tall for that small room. He was long and languid and his hair was in danger of being snagged by the wooden shelves full of crockery that poked out from the wall.

'Mi remember where yuh live,' he smiled. 'Mi kno yuh wudda cum hyah.'

He looked directly at me and his face said – *you know how to survive the worst of times and I trusted you'd look after my little brother, just like you did your dad.*

Mom was already brewing tea. It steamed as she poured it into a big brown pot. Our dog Tiny snuffled round everyone's feet until Lincoln tripped over him, nearly bashing his head on one of the shelves. Mom took Tiny by the collar and said, 'Sorry, sweetheart, you are going to 'ave to take a bit of fresh air. Ta-ra a bit,' and chucked him outside. Frigid air breathed into the kitchen, then the door snapped shut. Mrs Miller looked mightily relieved.

Mom told us what she'd heard in the pub: 'Two explosions,' she said, 'and they aren't sure yet how many casualties. It's likely people have died. It's not confirmed, but looks like those bombs might have been planted by the IRA.'

Nobody spoke. The magnitude of the news sat inside a silence only disturbed by the clatter of teacups as she fetched them from the cupboard. It was a bit awkward, drinking tea with no table. That was still functioning as Dad's desk in his headquarters in the front room. We all managed by leaning across each other and placing our cups on the counter by the sink when we'd finished.

'How did the concert go?' said Mom sheepishly. I could tell she felt strange asking the question when something so benign had been eclipsed by something so tragic.

'It was good,' I said, trying to avoid what had now been gnawing away at my brain for hours, but which Lincoln voiced then on my behalf: 'Derek didn't turn up. Nobody's seen him. No one knows where 'e is.' We watched as Mom and Mrs Miller swapped glances. Their eyes were brimful of alarm that they were attempting to control.

'Have either of you got Derek's phone number?' Mom asked.

We shook our heads.

Dewain intervened. 'Di mawnin will bring peace. Yuh'll si,' he said reassuringly. With that, he said it was time to go. They had a mile to walk home yet and it was nearly one o'clock in the morning.

Mrs Miller fixed her hat to her head and buttoned up her bright green coat. She took hold of Mom's hands and said, 'Why not show di bwoy di photographs? Huh? It wi help him, yuh know.'

Mom said, 'Thank you, Rosi,' and the Millers set off into that bitter night.

*

As the front door closed, my eyes landed on the door to the front room. It was firmly shut. A tendril of anger grew from my stomach into my chest.

'I see Herman's Hermit ain't budged.'

Mom didn't laugh at my joke.

'About that,' said Mom, and she wavered in the hallway. She stared at me. 'Your friend's mom, Rosi, well I've had a good chat with her tonight... Luke, I know it's late and it's been a terrible night, but would you like some cocoa?'

I would never have slept anyway. My mind was still fizzing, trying to process everything that had happened. Mom sat me down in the kitchen.

'I think you might like to have a look at these?' She passed me an oblong biscuit tin. It was the one with Lisa Hagan in a boat. My heart skipped a beat. But why did Mom want me to look at biscuits? I would be much happier eating them. 'Open it!'

I prised off the lid. It was crammed full of black and white photographs. There were postcards too. I didn't recognise anything. There were young men in sailors' uniforms, large palm trees, colonial-looking buildings, ships, more buildings with flags on posts. Everything looked ancient. Whoever had taken these photographs had taken them aeons ago. I began to

Silver in the Quarter

turn them over and look on the back. In neat handwriting there were a few words and dates. *Australia 1949. Singapore 1950.*

I looked up at Mom bemused.

'What's this got to do with anything?' I asked.

Mom scooped up a photo of a large naval ship. It had HMS Centaur written along its side. 'This was one of the ships your dad was on,' she said. 'It was your Uncle Sid who taught him how to be a jeweller, before that he was in the navy.'

'Dad was a sailor?'

'Yes, Luke, he was. It was what he always wanted to be. We were at school together, you know? We weren't that much older than you when we started going out. We were only sixteen. He was a lovely young man. Very quiet. Gentle.'

The tin on my lap suddenly felt heavier.

'It was great for 'im at first. 'E travelled just as 'e had always dreamed. I missed 'im of course, but you sort of get used to it. When you 'ave a husband working for the forces you know they'll be away for a while but that they will come back.'

She stopped for a moment and drew her eyes from the windowpane she'd been staring at and looked directly at me.

"'E had to go to war, son,' she said and her voice sounded a bit strangled. 'It was called the Korean War. It wasn't very nice. 'E saw some 'orrible things.'

I would have liked to have held her hand then or maybe even hugged her. She looked bereft, but I was a thirteen-year-old boy who went to Witton Common. It was 1974. We just didn't do things like that. So I stared at her instead.

'I received a telegram. I was being asked to visit a sanatorium in Scotland. I didn't quite know what was going on. Anyway, I travelled all the way up there and somehow found the place. This snotty official-looking man in a uniform told me to go to Ward 8 when I said who I was. It took me ages to find it. I walked in and there were about a dozen men lying like corpses in beds. I walked up and down looking for your dad but I couldn't find 'im, so I went and got that snotty chap and said that my husband was not on Ward 8. 'E turned round to me and said, 'Oh but Mrs Holden, he is,' and then 'e took me back and walked me to this bed, to this man I didn't recognise with a shaved head and red skin, all small, and eyes staring up at the ceiling...'

'And that was Dad wasn't it?'

She nodded.

Silver in the Quarter

She took the tin from me and began to fish around searching for something.

'This was your dad when 'e was young. 'E'd have been about eighteen there.'

She gave me a photograph and I was looking at a confident young man with handsome cheekbones, wearing a sailor's uniform.

'It's war, you see, son,' she said, 'it does terrible things.'

*

The next morning after only three hours' sleep I got up determined to go to school. It was Friday 22nd November. I needed to find out what had happened to Derek. As soon as I got there we were all bundled in to the hall where the headteacher, Mr Jackson, had called an assembly.

Mr Jackson stood sternly on the stage, impatiently watching us file in and sit down on the hard wooden chairs. After a hymn accompanied on piano by a very worn-out-looking Mr Arrowsmith, Mr Jackson spoke:

'As you will have heard by now there was a devastating incident that happened last night in the centre of Birmingham. Sadly there have been fatalities and there are a significant number of people seriously ill in hospital. We do not know how many exactly as yet. The police believe that the bombs were planted by the IRA. A third bomb was discovered on the Hagley Road, but fortunately this bomb did not go off. People in this school will undoubtedly have been affected by this tragedy. If that is the case, I would like to say that all of the staff here at Witton Common pass on their commiserations. This is undoubtedly a very difficult time for us all.'

All the time Mr Jackson was speaking I was trying to look around to see if I could see Derek. Across the way I spotted Lincoln doing exactly the same thing. I shrugged my shoulders. Lincoln shrugged back.

We had maths first lesson. Derek's chair was empty. I didn't hear a word that the maths teacher Mr Brigson said that whole lesson. I wanted to know where Derek was, but Mr Brigson only spoke the language of maths. If you weren't using words like hypotenuse or equilateral triangle, he would stare at you as though you were speaking in Vulcan. The bell rang for break. I ran to the music room. Mr Arrowsmith was searching through a box of percussion instruments on the floor. The triangles were tangled together and he was pulling them out in small heaps and wanging them on the floor like a child searching for a toy.

''Scuse me, sir.' Mr Arrowsmith ignored me. 'Mr Arrowsmith,' I spoke a bit louder now to counteract the cacophony of the percussion being thrown around.

Mr Arrowsmith looked at me impatiently. I saw that the whites of his eyes were threaded with tiny red veins.

'What is it, Luke?'

'Have you seen Derek O'Malley this morning, sir?'

'Haven't you heard? Derek O'Malley is still at the hospital. He was there last night.'

Of course when he said that I immediately thought the worst. It turned out, however, that Derek was in the hospital for a very different reason.

Derek arrived at lunchtime, looking similar to us: worn out. But his story couldn't have been more different.

The three of us convened in the music room. Derek explained how he and his mom and dad were about to leave for the concert at the Town Hall when his older sister's husband flew round the corner of their cul-de-sac in a right state. Derek's sister Chrissy had gone into labour. They didn't have a phone, so Chrissy had sent her husband to her mom and dad's house. Consequently, they had all squeezed into Derek's dad's Cortina (including a wailing Chrissy) and they had gone to the hospital together. Of course, they intended to drop Chrissy there and go on to the concert, but it hadn't quite worked out like that. Chrissy had kept shouting at her husband, then asking for her mother. Derek's dad wouldn't leave the hospital without his wife and in short they had all ended up staying there until Chrissy had given birth to a 7lb 8oz. baby girl at 9.22 this morning.

'Just think,' Derek said, buoyed up by a new sense of grandiosity, 'I am the cool uncle now, the one my niece will look up to for the rest of her life.'

'God 'elp that poor bab,' said Lincoln, rolling his eyes.

The fact that Derek was safe and the happy news that his sister had given birth to a healthy baby girl were the only glimpses of light in a Birmingham that was now in mourning. Grief and misery soon began to be shadowed by a gloomy paranoia that I had only witnessed in Dad during his worst episodes. Twenty-one

Silver in the Quarter

people were dead and one hundred and eighty-two injured. Derek soon understood that it was wise to shelve the Irish Eamonn Andrews accent that he often used to diffuse conflict. The whiff of an Irish brogue could now be the blue touchpaper to light a fire of fury. This was not a good time or place to be Irish.

Hours after the bombings, six Irishmen were arrested and kept in custody. Derek's dad said he might have been arrested himself simply for having an Irish accent had he not had such a solid alibi. He'd been in the hospital all night with his pregnant daughter. Derek began to sign his name Derek Malley, omitting the O, on all his exercise books. There were certain people looking for blood, wanting revenge. Chrissy, who had intended to have her baby baptised Aislin, changed her mind and christened her Janet.

Over the next few days stories about those who had been killed or injured shaped the news: young people on the brink of marriage, hardworking men who were having a pint at the end of a tough week, friends who'd been on holiday, lovers, daughters, husbands, fathers, sisters, mothers, aunties and uncles, friends, neighbours. Hurt or dead. Lives destroyed or damaged. Minds twisted with grief, pain and fear. There were at least a dozen kids at our school whose relatives had been at The Mulberry Bush and The Tavern in the Town that night. Some had survived, others hadn't. A girl in the year below us was the niece of the copper who had discovered the bomb that didn't explode. It had been placed in the doorway of a bank on the Hagley Road. He had prodded that bomb with his truncheon. His was the story of a miracle in some people's eyes, or pure unadulterated luck in others'.

Alongside this, things were still bad at home too. Dad continued to hole himself up in the front room. He had stopped going to work. Mom looked drained. She was working at Forgings and Pressworks during the day and doing shifts in the pub at night. The last thing we needed was for Mom to get ill, so of course she did. She took to bed with flu and within days Dad had the same. It took Mom five days to recover but Dad's illness went on and on. The front room became a drum in which a rhapsody of coughing persisted night and day. It rattled through the house. Even though Mom and I attempted to talk to him when he would come into the kitchen like a shuffling apparition, to get a glass of water, a slice of bread, he refused to speak to us.

Silver in the Quarter

*

It was the second week of December and Mom had had enough. She picked up the phone three times and then on the fourth attempt I heard her say, 'For God's sake, Mrs Brentwood, I'm sure your Tony's hernia is a cross to bear, but will you bloody well get off the line, I have an emergency call to make.'

The doctor who turned up a few hours later was a young man in spectacles wearing a neat, tweed suit. He had an air of newness, like an unopened milk bottle delivered fresh to your doorstep. Mom ushered him into the kitchen and I could hear her mumbling to him, attempting to explain why Dad had barricaded himself in the front room. I heard her say, 'No, Doctor, he hasn't been taking his medication.'

Perhaps it was the optimism of being newly qualified that gave him the patience to wait. He talked calmly to the closed door, reassuring Dad that he could help him.

'Your chest must be hurting a great deal, Mr Holden. What a terrible nuisance for you,' and 'I understand you don't want my help, but I shall just wait here until you are ready. There's no rush.'

After an hour Dad actually began to communicate and after another half an hour the front room door opened and Dad allowed him in. The doctor was in there for ages.

Later that night Mom said to me, 'I do believe there are some living saints.' The doctor had managed to get Dad to begin taking a course of antibiotics and the medication he needed for his nerves. He did not, however, manage to get Dad to remove his hat.

*

It was the last week of school. The rigid curriculum started to be relaxed. Mr Arrowsmith's lessons became uproarious sessions of belting out daft Christmas songs and carols while he tinkled out accompaniments on the piano. The pop group Mud had been on *Top of the Pops* singing 'Lonely this Christmas' and Derek, Lincoln and me did an impromptu version to Karen Dalby and her mates one lunchtime in the music room. Lisa Hagan smiled at me all the way through and twisted a tangle of her fiery mane with her elegant fingers. All the girls clapped and laughed at the end. I realised I was truly in love with Lisa Hagan and knew I had to do something about it.

The answer was there when I returned home that evening. I went up to my bedroom and found on my pillow a small black cardboard box. When I opened it, there was one of the silver lockets Dad and I had made weeks ago. It was resting on a mound of ruby-red velvet. I guess this was Dad's way of saying thank you to me for helping him. It was a gesture which showed me that his health was improving.

I took it out and opened the tiny clasp. The oval space that could accommodate a picture was empty. I shut it again and held it in my hand. An idea began to grow in my mind like a drop of ink spreading through water. I would never wear that locket. It was far too girly. Besides, Dad had loads of them. If Dad was going to give me a present, I'd much rather have a cassette radio. I'd been leaving hints for ages by circling several different compact cassettes in the Kays catalogue and leaving it open on that page. I had double circled the Philips one because you could add a microphone and sing into it and I longed to tape the charts countdown from the radio on a Sunday.

This locket needed to be worn by a girl. This locket belonged on the silky skin of Lisa Hagan. The idea thrilled me. I knew nothing of romance but this appeared to be a very romantic thing to do. I could get a picture of myself taken at the photo booth in Woolworths and put it inside.

The locket grew warm in my hand. I realised I'd been clutching it hard as I'd been thinking. Perhaps the photo idea was a bit too obvious. I desired to apply some mystery to my giddy ardour.

Then it came to me. I would snip off a clip of my hair with the nail scissors and put it inside the locket. I would drop it into her bag while she wasn't looking. I sat on my bed grinning at the subtle poetry of my idea.

Rosi Miller sent a thick, sticky ginger cake via Lincoln for Mom. Mom sent a fruit cake as heavy as a brick, wrapped in tin foil, to give to Lincoln for Rosi. Both were trimmed with identical blue tinsel. The table appeared in the kitchen again and our front room was back in commission. Now I was relieved to see that we might actually be able to sit around the table and have Christmas dinner. Things were getting back on track. Dad went to work for a day and returned with a Christmas card from Eric and Sandeep. Sandeep or

Eric had written in scrawly writing: *Get well soon, mate, Happy Christmas. Say hello to Luke.* I touched the inside of the card and a filmy residue of sparkling dust clung to my fingertips.

I took the boxed locket into school every day that week but did not have the courage to complete my secret mission. I had no sense at all that for a young girl to discover an anonymous silver locket in her bag containing a tuft of mousey-brown hair might be a bit creepy. Not a bit of it. I did not tell Lincoln or Derek of my lionhearted gallantry. Derek would have laughed and called me a sappy twat. No, this was something I needed to accomplish alone.

On the final Friday, we were being allowed to go home after lunch. I seized the moment and sat next to Lisa Hagan in the dinner hall. My palms were sweating. Her bag was on the floor. It was now or never. I pretended to tie the lace on my shoe and deftly shoved the love gift into the bottom of her bag. She was oblivious, too busy arm-wrestling with Derek at the table edge and laughing her head off when he won, saying, 'Good game, good game' like Bruce Forsyth, with his chin sticking in the air.

That was the last I ever saw of that silver locket. It never appeared on Lisa Hagan's swanlike throat and she never spoke of it to anyone, as far as I know. I could never ask, because to do so would be to reveal my love for her, which I never could. I do not know to this day whether she ever even found the box. It may have rolled out of her bag. She could have thrown it in the bin. Who would blame her once she'd found the ratty hair tangled inside.

I took that silver locket for granted. Dad made so many of them, casually sold them under the table in pubs for booze money. I had made hundreds alongside him. The abundance made me think that there would always be plenty. When I came to look years later, there was not one left. Now, I do not possess one of Dad's lockets. It would be good to have one to open every so often, like a door to the past.

Perhaps Lisa Hagan still possesses that shiny silver case, the size of a sixpence, that was crafted by a father and son, one cold Saturday in the Jewellery Quarter. Perhaps she kept it somewhere safe and when she was older handed it down to her own children. That is what I would hope for. The lock of hair will now be dust.

Silver in the Quarter

*

Courage continued to elude me. I never directly asked Lisa Hagan to go out with me and over the next three years stood by and watched as she dated: Keith Duggan, Tommy Clitheroe, Moses Lee, Terry Shoemacker, and Gerard Stipes. She also snogged Derek one night after a school disco. I wasn't happy about that, although I wasn't annoyed for very long as my eyes were by then set on Karen Dalby.

*

On Christmas Eve 1974 Derek O'Malley, Lincoln Miller and me went into Birmingham. The last hours to shop before the big day. We caught the bus together and jangled with laughter on the top deck amidst the fug of cigarette smoke, writing our names in the dribbling, steamy windows. It was freezing cold, but the three of us wore bomber jackets. Now we wouldn't be seen dead in duffel coats. What we looked like and what we wore was becoming an obsession to us. In those few short weeks we had changed. It was as though all the events that had taken place had accelerated the ageing of every cell in our bodies. We were new. Different. Older. The results were as potent as a spell cast in a fairy tale. Now the city centre of Birmingham was familiar to us. That night of the concert had galvanised us. The terrorist attack had been like those machine presses in Dad's workshop. We had been flattened but we were malleable and strong, just like those tough sheets of silver metal. We were being formed into resilient shields. We shone. The light glanced off each one of us and reflected on one another. We walked together in a defiant solidarity, our flares flapping in the wind, our hands stuffed into pockets.

I would like to be able to say that we were such thoughtful kids we had saved our pocket money and were on a mission to buy our moms' Christmas presents or that we were on our way to help out at the vagrants' mission. No. My preoccupations were much more self-serving. I had this notion that in making the trip into the centre of Birmingham, I was going to bump into Lisa Hagan. In my fantasy she would be wearing the locket, she would see me in the street and run up to me and thank me, saying, 'I knew it was from you. I recognised the lock of hair. You are my hero.' Derek and Lincoln would be standing there, mouths open, incredulous at my magnetic attraction to the female sex. Of course, that didn't happen,

Silver in the Quarter

although it didn't stop me from continuously rubbernecking any young girl about our age who vaguely resembled Lisa.

Lincoln was also on a mission. He was determined to go and buy an LP called *Catch a Fire* by Bob Marley and the Wailers. The band no longer looked like the dapper young men that I'd seen on the cover of the record I'd chosen from Dewain's collection. Now Bob Marley's hair was a mane of wild dreadlocks and his clothes were flowing shirts and bell-bottomed jeans. Lincoln had been saving for ages to get this record. It spoke of slavery, freedom, love. He was following in his brother's footsteps as a record collector. He was going to take me and Derek to a shop that specialised in reggae music. The money in his pocket was itching to be exchanged for those shiny discs. That music was Lincoln's rapture. The cacophony of horror that we had heard that night after the concert was soothed away by the mighty medicine of that sound. Lincoln was striding the pavement of city centre Birmingham with an absorbed intent he would never lose.

I looked up and around me as we walked. Having a dad like mine and knowing now that catastrophe can be a breath away, made me hyper alert to my surroundings: naked bulbs were strung high on black cord across the shops, plastic yellow Christmas crackers sat in the centre of each string like oversized toffees, department store windows were glass tanks housing frosted Christmas trees, the floors strewn with wiggling snakes of tinsel, gaudy baubles. Streams of shoppers moved around me with multiple bags and worried eyebrows.

The Salvation Army was singing 'Good King Wenceslas' and rattling tins for donations. We stopped and joined in, singing loudly and out of tune. Once it was clear we had made a nuisance of ourselves we strolled away, cackling like crows.

As we walked toward the record shop, I recognised the location from that Saturday Dad had first brought me into the city centre. We were up on St Chad's Circus right by the Catholic cathedral.

'This way!' I said, making a quick detour.

Lincoln groaned and shouted, 'Warmsy, where you off to?'

'There's something I wanna show you. It won't take long.' I knew Derek would love it. Then we came to a place where light flitted like a summer lake across a colourful expanse.

It was the Mo Zayic.

Silver in the Quarter

*

''Ave a good look, Derek. You won't believe it. The whole thing is made up of thousands of little tiles.'

Derek stopped and stared at it. Next thing, he's scrambling up and tightrope-walking the thin wall around a pond of water in front of it. I watched him stretch his body to reach it. He scrutinised the image pressing his nose to the wall, then running his fingers across the tiles like he was reading Braille. He turned to us beaming like he was Alexander Fleming and he'd just discovered penicillin.

'Ah skill. It must have taken ages to do that. Solid or wha'?'

Lincoln pointed to the crowd in the picture. Their hands reaching upwards.

'Why are all those brethren lookin' up to the man with the miserable face?'

'Oh 'e's John F. Kennedy. 'E was the President of the United States of America. 'E's probably not very 'appy cos he knows what's coming. 'E got shot in the 'ead after that.'

'What's it say?' Lincoln was shifting from one foot to another trying to read the writing in the panels down the side. I hadn't been able to see it properly last time.

I read it out loud:

> 'There are
> no white or
> coloured
> signs on
> the grave-
> yards of
> battle.'

It was a curious way to express something important.

'Some of our teachers call black kids "coloured", don't they?' observed Derek. He was back with us on the pavement, having teetered his way round the edge of the water.

'That's cos they're old and a bit dunce bat,' said Lincoln.

We stood motionless staring at it. For some strange reason, I thought about Dad and how he never took his hat off. Then I thought about that old black and white photograph of him in his sailor's uniform when he was eighteen years old.

'Can we go and get those records now?' pleaded Lincoln.

Silver in the Quarter

A steely gust of wind hurled itself at us and we zipped our bomber jackets right close to our necks to keep out the cold. We walked against a gust of winter air that howled into our open faces and headed towards the music.

In the Ape's Shadow

Stewart Lee

STEWART LEE grew up in Solihull and began stand-up in 1988 at the age of 20, having been inspired by seeing the post-punk anti-comic Ted Chippington open for The Fall in Birmingham in 1984. He won the Hackney Empire new act of the year award in 1990 and for the next dacede was a five-nights-a-week regular on the stand-up circuit. In 2001 he was asked to contribute to the libretto for the composer Richard Thomas' *Jerry Springer: The Opera*, which went on to win four Olivier awards. His most recent stand-up shows have been Stand Up Comedian (2004), 90s Comedian (2005), 41st Best Stand-up Ever (2007), If You Prefer a Milder Comedian, Please Ask for One (2009), Carpet Remnant World (2012) and Content Provider (2016). Stewart Lee's *Comedy Vehicle*, featuring his stand-up, ran for four series on BBC2, and won the BAFTA for Best Comedy Programme in 2012. Stewart is also the author of the stand-up comedy studies *How I Escaped My Certain Fate* (2010) and *If You Prefer a Milder Comedian Please Ask for One* (2012). He has written for *The Wire*, *Uncut*, the *Observer* and *Mojo*, and won *Celebrity Mastermind* answering questions on the guitarist Derek Bailey. Stewart has two children and has lived in Stoke Newington, Hackney, since the 1990s. He recently recorded a half-hour piece inspired by his contribution to this book, *Telly Savalas Looks At Birmingham*, with the free-jazz trio Capri-Batterie.

THE IRISH REPUBLICAN Army's simultaneous bombing of two Birmingham city centre pubs took place on 21 November 1974, killing twenty-one young people, drinking and laughing in a pre-punk Midland demi-monde of denim flares and crimpled hair and warm brown beer served in jam jar glasses, and everyone smelling pungently protohuman in those long ago no-deodorant days of once-a-week baths and manual labour.

It is heartbreaking to imagine; soft seventies bodies blown clean through the brickwork, back before we reluctantly accepted terrorism as a fact of life. There was still a hippy boutique holding out against the encroaching future on New Street, stylised to look like a stuccoed psychedelic cave, but the Swinging Sixties were officially over. Birmingham was now in the dark swirling centre of the Semtex

Seventies, and urban guerillas had bombs in their cellars.

Six and a half years earlier, in the spring of 1968, I made landfall, 'a little bonny boy' according to the handwritten notes on the adoption charity paperwork, in an orphanage in Lichfield, an unprofitable bastard by-catch from one of the many unplanned enthusiasms of The Summer of Love.

My saviours were a kind and caring couple that fitted the Church of England Children's Society's ideal parental criteria, who lived five minutes' walk beyond the Birmingham city boundary, a world away from the Welsh Marches where I had gestated in conspiratorial silence, and then finally first drawn breath in a hospital that has since been demolished, as if to obliterate all traces of my arrival in the area.

Eighteen years later, I left home bound for London, rarely to return, as those whose love would have drawn me back to Birmingham slowly died or disappeared, as people do, leaving me alone, without brothers or sisters, but with three caskets of ashes to tend intermittently on significant dates, in a cemetery just inside the city's edge. My grandmother, my grandfather, and my mother. The people who raised me.

Perhaps I have no right to lay any claim to

In the Ape's Shadow

Birmingham. I had been merely passing through the Midlands, it appears, from somewhere west where I was unwanted, to somewhere east where I was unknown. But the accents and attitudes of my mother and her parents, who met on the shop floor of the Cadbury's chocolate factory between the wars, were formed by Birmingham, and I grew up in their shadow, and in the shadow of the second city, the only city I knew.

And in the shadow of an enormous ape.

The Birmingham pub bombings, amongst other things, had permanently disrupted my grandmother's weekly routine. She was an enthusiastic lifelong weekly participant in Spot the Ball, a contest involving marking with a cross the supposed position of a football that had been surgically removed from the damp sky of a grainy black and white photograph of a football game. It appeared in the *Birmingham Evening Mail*, then Britain's largest selling local newspaper.

The name of the competition was of course illogical. Entrants were not being invited to 'spot' the ball at all, as the ball was not visible. They were being invited instead to suggest a position the ball might have occupied, perhaps by looking at the eyelines of the shaggy-haired sex-faced players pictured.

In the mid-seventies over three million people a week played this nationally syndicated ball-imagining game. Now the figure stands at less than fourteen thousand, and the jackpot of £250,000 has not been paid out for over a decade. Yet still a dwindling brigade of dedicated ball-imaginers imagine on.

My grandmother was keen to win the competition, which she always studied at length on the day it appeared, canvassing my grandfather for his considered opinion. She chose to hand-deliver her entry each week to the actual offices of the newspaper, thinking this would in some way increase her chances of imagined invisible ball victory.

The concrete edifice of The Post and Mail building in Colmore Circus, to which Nan made her pilgrimage every week with me in tow, was subsequently demolished in 2005, as the city systematically erased all traces of the architectural style that had seen it nationally ridiculed.

The implausible but real 1980 promotional film, *Telly Savalas Looks at Birmingham*, features a voice-over recorded by the lollipop-sucking Kojak actor, who never visited Birmingham, eulogising the 'nations's industrial powerhouse – you feel like you've been projected into the twenty-first century' – over panoramic shots of monolithic futurist landscapes.

Inexplicably, a substantial part of *Telly Savalas Looks at Birmingham* is made up of footage of an outdoor over-fortys disco competition. 'Birmingham's roads are revolutionary,' waxes the crazy baldhead, 'a four-mile circuit of dual carriageways, tunnels and overpasses, linking up with the main arteries of the city and the Aston Expressway.'

The bus into town pushed up the Stratford Road from the top of my nan's street, through neighbourhoods familiar to her as a younger woman, now colonised by the Asian community, the road lined with saree shops and exotic food outlets. In Sparkhill we would peep out of the top deck to look down a particular side road, to see if my grandfather's old sky blue Ford Cortina, which had the smiling headlamps and friendly radiator grille face of all seventies cars, was still parked there.

An Indian family had arrived at the house to buy it second-hand the previous year, in a deputation of half a dozen, the male elders proffering rolls of used notes my grandparents insisted smelt of mothballs. Though my grandparents had been to Portugal, where the hole-in-the-ground toilets had disappointed my nan, they displayed nonetheless a kind of hysteria about interacting with such unfamiliar visitors. And then, immediately after the buyers' departure, the sitting room was hoovered, and the sofa cushion covers washed, lest Hindu moth eggs from the subcontinent should hatch and wreak havoc upon the fabrics of pest-free homes, just beyond the borders of the infested city.

Once, I saw the old car from the bus, actually in motion, needling through the traffic in front of us. It had borne us west to the Welsh picnic sites of Brummies' cheese and tomato sandwich dreams, Lake Vyrnwy or Llangollen. What a different life it must now be experiencing, in the heavy harness of its city duties, doubtless ferrying headscarved grandmothers between religious observances, its cheerful face still smiling.

In Digbeth, opposite the Town Hall and the medieval timber-framed Old Crown pub, the bus would rear up high into the air over the rickety rattling rollercoaster frame of the Camp Hill Flyover, an excitable temporary traffic-calming structure thrown up in a mid-sixties weekend, that eventually hung on for twenty-six tenacious years. Again! Again! The Camp Hill Flyover! Again!

In the Ape's Shadow

After the space-age-illuminated signs of the Bull Ring shopping centre – one a pint pot of bubbling bitter endlessly emptying and refilling in an invitation to alcoholism in adulthood – we would alight. And it was a point on our walk, from the bus stop to the Birmingham Mail office itself, that I always looked forward to the most. And it's a memory that I am going to use as a central prop to support the entire subtext of this memoir, Atlas buckling under the weight of the half-remembered world.

Each week we would traverse the landscaped Eden of Manzoni Gardens, a grass and concrete open space, named after the city engineer and surveyor Sir Herbert Manzoni. Manzoni once declared, 'I have never been very certain as to the value of tangible links with the past. They are often more sentimental than valuable. There is little of real worth in Birmingham's architecture. Future generations will be better occupied in applying their thoughts and energies to forging ahead, rather than looking backward.' He then went on to bulldoze the city centre, the old library and the original Bull Ring market hall.

Today Manzoni Gardens too is gone, demolished in a subsequent city centre upgrade, Herbert Manzoni style. I can't even work out where the square used to be, as it seems to have been sucked up into the retooled entrance of New Street station. But in March 1973, when I was four years old, it was in Manzoni's now Lost Garden of Birmingham that I first set eyes upon a statue that was to stay with me forever.

Higher than a house, it seemed to me, and in the form of a great black roaring ape, its fists raised in anger, its red mouth raw with rage. All around its feet, disgruntled Brummies tutted and moaned, cursing it as an ugly waste of money that could have been better spent elsewhere, the distinctively downbeat speech patterns perfectly machine-tooled for the task of disparaging an inanimate monster ape. 'Bloody stupid ugly bloody thing.'

When I started out in the pub attics and back rooms of the nascent stand-up circuit in London in the autumn of 1989, I found myself stifling the traces of those same nasal inflections, loaded as they were with expectations. I fabricated more neutral tones, anxious to escape the assumption that I would be a regional comic addressing regional themes. Liverpudlians stole. Scotsmen fought. Geordies walked out in frozen snow wearing only vests of string and endurance. And in the popular imagination, Brummies were Bennies, named after the river-dwelling bobble-hat odd-job man of ATV's seventies *Crossroads* soap opera. At the same time as dissolving prejudice around learning difficulties, Benny had also helped to solidify a stereotype of Birmingham folk as good-natured semiaquatic simpletons, incapable of either malice or cunning.

The young Frank Skinner, who I'd seen in a late night cabaret in Edinburgh in the summer of 1989, and had assumed correctly was bound for glory, had his hometown's speech patterns sewn up anyway. The Rabelaisian intricacies of his deftly described obscenities were rendered charmingly inoffensive and profoundly ridiculous by the guileless quality of his dialect.

I forget the rest of Frank's best routine at the time, but the punchline involved a kangaroo, with a perfectly inappropriate Birmingham accent, repeating hilariously over and over again the increasingly agitated request, 'I said, can I have some leaves please?'

And so, as I scraped through late eighties try-out stage-times in Balham and Clapham South and Clapham North and Clapham Common and Crouch End and Acton, my identifying tones were deliberately diminished. I was an ambitious Peter denying his

Birmingham Christ, a Birmingham Christ with peas and faggots and gravy all down his divided garments.

The cock crowed three times, like the siren of the chocolate factory sounding out over Bourneville Lane, and before I knew it I was without an accent, the vowel sounds of my childhood reserved now for unfiltered expressions of rage, joy or sexual arousal.

So what am I now? A building without obvious foundation, buffeted by billowing fortune, a tree without roots. I am like a cabbage in this society.

To be fair, the Birmingham that formed me, and my family, is no more. To me, it is a memory, sealed in a buried time capsule, a mountaintop cairn made from broken Cadbury staff shop chocolate biscuits, terrorist bombs, and long-lost public sculptures; dead aunties' attics and audacious traffic-calming measures; now closed comic-book stores and punk rock record shops in demolished subways; Birmingham bands I never saw in licensed premises that would have ejected me; and unsung Birmingham artists and writers I could have met and never did, whose influence and possible friendship I missed by mere moments. Birmingham left me no option but to leave.

Years after departing, I realised how close I was to a Birmingham counterculture I could have submerged

In the Ape's Shadow

myself in. From exposure to their first album, 1982's *Pigs on Purpose*, as a thirteen-year-old John Peel listener, I had always loved The Nightingales, a Birmingham post-punk band that mix rickety Captain Beefheart riffs and a krautrock pulse with literary sensibilities and a sometimes strange kind of blue-collar Nashville sentimentality.

I told the publishers of this book that this piece could be mainly about The Nightingales, and the Birmingham post-punk scene generally, but I've been worrying at it for months now and I can't seem to make it fit the brief I agreed to. The story keeps coming back to me, and what Birmingham means to me, as someone who left it at eighteen, and now understands it only through memory and music.

Perhaps the whole idea of this piece was based on a false premise. I was three years too young to pass for old enough to enter the places The Nightingales played in the early eighties, though I have a (possibly false) memory of waiting outside a Birmingham University gig at fifteen, and failing to gain admission because I didn't have an NUS card.

Though I had failed to see their early incarnations live, The Nightingales' 7" single sleeves were stencilled onto my school bag, when everybody else had Diamond Head, Iron Maiden, and Magnum, the Midlands' unassailable metal orthodoxy intact despite the punk wars.

As The Nightingales' last remaining original member Robert Lloyd, who beat Frank Skinner in vocalist auditions forty years earlier, said to me last month, 'I expect you were beaten up a lot on our account.' It was a kind thought, but I would have been beaten up anyway, with or without a school bag stencil of 'Paraffin Brain' b/w 'Elvis, the Last Ten Days'.

I still owe The Nightingales and their circle a vast debt. Exposure to their self-run record label's house alternative comedian Ted Chippington, opening for The Fall at The Powerhouse in Hurst Street in 1984, single-handedly set me on the road to stand-up. I thought you had to be a big personality to be a comedy performer. Ted, who occupied space and time with a hilariously confrontational absence of apparent ability or content, showed me all you needed was one joke and a bad attitude.

Now, long since gone from the city that shaped me but remaining sentimentally attached to it, I attempt to rebuild that old Birmingham in my memory, from the stories that remain within me, authenticated fragments to place in a sealed envelope for the benefit of my bewildered children, set down in stone before my circuits fade.

My first Birmingham memory, I think, is of those bombs. I remembered them again recently, as I tried to explain Westminster Bridge, and Manchester Arena, and London Bridge, and Grenfell Tower, and Finsbury Park to my own children, as confused by 2017's Summer of Tragedy as I was by the pub blasts forty-three years ago.

My second Birmingham memory is of a black stone beast, my exposure to it inextricably bound to the ebb and flow of the IRA campaign.

In the immediate aftermath of the pub bombings, Birmingham's Irish community were ostracised and assaulted. Anti-Irish sentiment spread across the whole country. Somehow, exceptions were made for the nice Irish doctor my mother worked for, the fact that he was from the Republic anyway being a nuance too far for most Midland minds.

I'd have been six years old but I remember it well, that mass hatred of the Irish, back before O'Neill's theme pubs, the notion of the craic, and how funny Dave Allen was joined forces in a psychic pincer movement to rehabilitate the whole Irish land mass in the eyes of the unconvinced Englishenvolk. In the end I married an Irishwoman, I think mainly as an elaborate apology, a debt now paid.

Ireland eventually drank the reluctant British mainland into an under the table accommodation in the eighties, as residual differences were set aside in a succession of plastic Paddy pubs, and the creamy foam of the Guinness became award-winning white wild horses, surging in the sea, in every Channel 4 commercial break.

Half a dozen blameless Irishmen, known later as The Birmingham Six, were swiftly imprisoned for the bombings. Justice had to be seen to be done.

In 1982, I saw Birmingham's feverish soul-punk seer, and former Killjoys frontman, Kevin Rowland relaunch Dexys Midnight Runners as a raggle-taggle Irish emigrant showband at the Hippodrome theatre on Hurst Street. It's worth remembering how raw and provocative that incarnation might have seemed in Rowland's still hurting hometown. Like Christ who came before him, Kevin Rowland embraced the outcasts. Rowland's latest album, 2016's superb *Let the Records Show – Dexys Do Irish Country and Soul*, still won't let those defiant Irish-Birmingham links drop.

Working back sixty years, 1950s BBC archives of

unaccompanied recordings of the elderly Birmingham folk singer Cecilia Costello document a workhouse woman, born in 1884 to parents who fled the famine, whose songs stumble majestically forth in the kind of rich Birmingham accent I haven't heard since my auntie Gladys died, whilst remaining unmistakably sourced from an Irish storehouse.

Upon the Birmingham Six's release, in March 1991, my grandmother steadfastly refused to believe they weren't responsible. 'They were up to something,' she insisted, but passed away before the men, who became the subject of a furiously slurred Pogues song, banned by broadcasters, received substantial financial compensation, a decade later.

'Why is your hair so grey?', she said to me, a few years later, in a care home near Malvern. 'And why are you so fat? How old are you? How old am I?'

The Birmingham Six's release also gave rise to a fantastic 1990s joke by the character comedian, an unsurpassed parody of agitprop punk orators by the stand-up Simon Munnery; 'The Birmingham Six are free! When will the rest of Birmingham be free?'

The three surviving IRA members, now confidentially agreed to be responsible for the Birmingham Pub Bombings, remain at large, two of them protected from prosecution by a subclause in the Good Friday Agreement. A memorial to their twenty-one victims lies in the grounds of Birmingham's bijou bonsai cathedral, St Philip's.

In the building's appropriately small shadow lies the grave of Little Nanetta Stocker, who died in 1819 and was, at thirty-three inches, the 'smallest woman ever in this kingdom'. When I took the children on a forced pilgrimage to my hometown last year, my five-year-old daughter stretched out upon the grass of the tiny woman's grave, purring with delight at Nanetta's doll-like diminutiveness, Edward Burne-Jones' stained glass burning cobalt blue behind us as pretty office girls manged Pret A Manger.

Beyond their fascination for Nanetta's grave, I was unable to inculcate much enthusiasm for the city of my childhood in my own children, who reacted with understandable embarrassment to my tearful waves of nostalgia as we wandered the now unrecognisably altered streets. At night this cathedral square ran with a river of rats, I remembered.

Finally, we stood and watched the dusty demolition of the architect John Madin's brutalist Central Library, in whose concrete precincts, in 1981, I was struck repeatedly about the head and face with a rolled umbrella 'for being a mod'. I wasn't even a mod. I just had a mod face.

John Madin, a Moseley-born concrete conjuror of the maligned post-war Birmingham reconstruction, regarded the library as one of his greatest achievements, but he died in 2012 without seeing his often despised buildings critically rehabilitated, with some of his works even saved for the nation by English Heritage.

Living through the shattering upheaval of the city's redesign must have been traumatic. I didn't interview anyone especially for this piece, but conversations I've had with people over the last six months, as I mulled this story over, have naturally been skewed to its proposed subject material. Over lunch in London's Chinatown last month I asked the free jazz saxophonist Evan Parker, who came to study botany in the city in 1962, about his memories of The Great Concreting.

'I think they had just built the inner ring road or maybe were still finishing it,' Evan remembers. 'There was much talk of all the great pubs that had been knocked down. So much was destroyed, just to make way for the motor car. But I remember the Diskery record shop and its owner Maurice. And the Elbow Room. We used to play before the rock band arrived.

Jim Capaldi was there. They were so indifferent to our music and the sensibilities of the few friends who came to listen to us that they used to leave the TV on at the other end of the bar. It's not much to salvage from four years.'

In Evan's mind, it seems Birmingham's indifference to the future pioneers of European Free improvisation is mirrored by its tolerance of concrete. Nonetheless, I have a terrible feeling that Madin's brutalist buildings, had the city committed to them and let subsequent waves of hostility wash over their mute and enduring forms, might have stood the test of time better than the novelty confectionary shapes of the city's current retail-outlet-driven redesign.

In the end, Birmingham will have to stop smashing itself to bits and continually upgrading. It's not an iPhone. The recurrent facelifts of the city centre are an endless stone and steel tournament of Stick or Twist, indecision writ large in each subsequent surge of shopping malls.

In the early seventies, until the point of my parents' sudden, and still shrouded, separation, we lived in a small terraced house in a leafy but modest estate of cul-de-sacs and open spaces in the Birmingham satellite settlement of Solihull. Sixties precincts were bodged unceremoniously onto its now fatally compromised medieval centre, and the High Anglican church tower of St Alphege loomed oppressively over the civic fountains, like a massive child-molesting choir master.

Tony Iommi from Black Sabbath was routinely chased around Mell Square on Saturday afternoons by denim-jacketed thirteen-year-old boys shouting, 'It's Tony Iommi from Black Sabbath!'. And yet, heroically, the half-fingered fret-shredder still chose to do his shopping in the square, trailing a snake train of teenage diabolists, like some kind of carrier-bag-toting Pied Piper of Death.

My mother had an argument with Maggie Moone, the cabaret artiste who sang the songs on Tom O'Connor's *Name That Tune*, over the wrongful acquisition of a shopping trolley in the same Sainsbury's that Iommi shopped in. Don Maclean, Peter Glaze's born-again Christian foil from the comedy sketches on BBCl's *Crackerjack*, was sometimes seen there. Bev Bevan of Electric Light Orchestra and their Brumbeat progenitors The Move was occasionally in evidence. Other than that, Solihull town centre in the seventies and eighties was consistently unglamorous.

My mother left home with me sometime in 1972,

I think, and while her divorce uncoiled I was moved into a narrow box room in my grandparents' house in nearby Shirley, the shelf behind the bed still stacked with my emigrated uncle's 1950s *Eagle* comics. I fell asleep nightly listening to Soviet-era Radio Moscow on a muffled transistor, staring for comfort at a lone framed picture of two furry fat white cats — neither of which could have been swung within that bedroom — which today hangs by my daughter's pillow.

My *Eagle*-reading uncle left for Canada in the late sixties, saying, probably correctly, that you couldn't get anywhere in Britain unless you had the right old-school tie. I ended up, through no fault of my own, owning one of those contested ties myself.

My uncle appears as an extra, playing a policeman, in the classic Birmingham-shot Peter Watkins 1967 film *Privilege*. The dystopian psychedelic satire of social control is also notable for its Patti Smith sampled soundtrack. Judicious freeze-framing of the newly released Blu-ray will locate my uncle, on two separate occasions, holding back hordes of fans from Paul Jones' proto-fascist pop star outside Birmingham Town Hall.

My uncle also maintains that the best live band he

ever saw as a teenager in Birmingham was not the much better known Kinks, but the city's own garage growlers, The Renegades, who, clad in Confederate uniforms, had a minor hit with an unattributed remake of Vince Taylor's 'Brand New Cadillac' in 1964, and then decamped to Helsinki, where they became the Finland Beatles, and then the Finland ELO.

The bassist from Birmingham's Beatle apprentices The Applejacks, Megan Davis, grew up on my grandparents' road, and I think my mother and her brother may have known her. As a kid, I remember my mum had all the sixties Applejacks singles, and the group seemed to exist in the collective folkloric consciousness as the local talent that nearly made it.

When I bought my mum a CD reissue of The Applejacks' back catalogue, in 1990, thinking I had found the perfect Christmas present, she seemed to have no memory of the group at all, and the gift was swiftly filed away in the attic. In the end I gave it to my emigrated uncle, though he seemed unsure whether he should accept it or not, perhaps fearing nostalgic feelings for the land he had bravely left in an act of class war.

Having come north-east to Birmingham at the turn of the twentieth century, from locations in rural

Worcestershire, forgotten by all surviving family members, my grandparents had finally made a permanent home in Shirley, where I now lived with them, a quarter of a mile outside the boundaries of the city, having escaped to its suburbs just before World War II.

But my grandfather still remembered mustard-gas-blind soldiers, back from World War I, walking in crocodile formation, their eyes bound with bandages, their hands on each other's shoulders, on the platform of Snow Hill station. And being beaten for being left-handed. And living so near to Cadbury's that he lay in bed until the siren sounded and then sprinted to his position on the production line through the closing gates.

I remember meeting a great-grandmother once, known as Old Nan, a vast blue bulk sat near the window at the top of a Birmingham tower block, as I lay on the floor staring at her big black orthopaedic shoe. But perhaps I have imagined this.

One of my grandfather's brothers, a navvy who worked on the expanding A-road network, joined Oswald Mosley's British Union of Fascists in the thirties and eventually disappeared from Birmingham to Canada. But mine was not a family of Nazis. Reg, as

I think he was known, was very much the blackshirt of the family.

My adopted grandfather stood in, perhaps unwittingly, as a father figure to me when I was little, but my Marvel comics confused him and he told me he thought that sitting inside and drawing and writing, instead of playing football outside, was 'what nancy boys do'. When I got a place at university he warned me not to learn so much that 'I went doolally, like these professors on TV'.

My grandfather rarely spoke of his war experiences working as an engineer on Lancaster bombers. But once, and once only, he all but wept as he recalled flying over the ravaged city of Dresden, soon after the firebombing. My grandmother was unsympathetic to the Germans who had perished in their thousands. She remembered nights spent without her husband, scurrying up the garden in the flak light to the shelter with her children, as the skies of Birmingham and Coventry burned. He told her she didn't know what she was talking about. Nothing was moving, except a dog.

But my grandfather's humanitarianism had its limits. Once, I remember, when I was three or four, he drove me around Handsworth just to show me where the 'jungle bunnies and coons' lived, telling me to remember that Enoch, whose 1968 'Rivers of Blood' speech was routinely referred to by anxious Brummies as if it were a prediction of biblical proportions, was right.

That said, this language reflected the values of the time, and was ubiquitous in TV comedy shows and family Christmas dinners. Pubs politely advised 'No Blacks, No Irish, No Dogs.' Today the same sentiments are expressed by tabloids and Tories in more sanitised terms, but they are the same sentiments nonetheless.

Indeed, as late as 1983 I actually appeared in a school production of Agatha Christie's as yet unrenamed *Ten Little Niggers*! There were black children in our school!! All the women in the show were boys in dresses!!! The kid playing the fisherman went on to be in Napalm Death!!!! It was the recent past and it was nuts.

But back then, peering out of Granddad's car, I remember thinking the brightly painted house fronts of Birmingham's burgeoning Afro-Caribbean community looked brilliant, shining out in the shabby streets, blossoming on the fringes of still abandoned

World War II bombsites. We snowflakes are born, and not made, it appears.

And, years later in 1982, when John Peel's stand-in Mark Ellen played a 1978 BBC radio session recording of 'Handsworth Revolution' by Birmingham's British reggae pioneers Steel Pulse, it belatedly made historical sense of what I'd been presented with as a child. A year previously, I had listened to the Police radio frequency under the covers, as riots mushroomed out of Handsworth, and made their way towards us.

> *We once beggars are now choosers*
> *No intention to be losers*
> *Striving forward with ambition*
> *And if it takes ammunition*
> *We rebel in Handsworth revolution.*

By the end of the seventies, for a generation of kids, multicultural bands like Birmingham's The Beat and the Two Tone crew from Coventry made racism seem just impossibly naff, like something some kind of dick would believe in. I moved into early adolescence and I know those defiantly cross-cultural recordings definitely helped discredit the casual, and not so casual, racism of the world I grew up in.

In the mid-seventies, when a man in my grandparents' street was planning to sell his house to a black family, an unofficial vigilante deputation of neighbours took it upon themselves to counsel him against it. I remember, as a precocious little boy, telling everyone that I thought that what those people had done was wrong. Perhaps I was just virtue signalling, already a six-year-old libtard.

Eventually I was reassured by adults who knew about these things that those wanting to stop the black family moving in weren't concerned about race in and of itself, but were worried about protecting the financial value of the houses. If one went, they would all go, apparently. And then everyone in Shirley may as well not have bought their way one mile out of Birmingham.

Within a few decades the same street was fairly, and functionally, multicultural. Nobody died. The changing face of the city caught up with its outward-bound escapees in the end. And if their attitudes seem brutal, it was only a decade earlier that Conservative MP Peter Griffiths won the seat of Smethwick, legitimising people's prejudices with the slogan, 'If you want a nigger for a neighbour, vote Liberal or Labour.'

In the Ape's Shadow

From its suburban seventies fringes, the city, its history, its filth, its planning chaos, its cultural jumble, seemed like something my family were pleased to be free of. In 1988, when the National Trust chose to preserve for the nation the last of the 'back-to-back' slum housing in Inge Street and Hurst Street, I remember my grandmother was angry and confused by the decision. Why were they saving the Birmingham that she and her generation had wanted to forget and leave behind? We had moved on, hadn't we?

Similarly, when their first colour television arrived, in 1974, my grandmother steadfastly refused henceforth to watch anything in black and white, even classic old movies that she had loved. 'We've paid for colour,' she would say. But ironically, if anyone 'coloured' came on the colour television, she would change the channel. Not all colour was welcome.

Even Ken Boothe's 1974 *Top of the Pops* performance of the solid gold reggae classic, now one of my all-time favourite singles, 'Everything I Own', was switched off in horror halfway through, when Ken began canoodling with another 'coloured'. 'I think we'll have it off now.' Today the same Trojan single is a mainstay of my vintage Wurlitzer jukebox. Ken wins.

I have an old picture book, a hopeful and prescriptive tract entitled *Our Birmingham: The Birmingham of Our Forefathers and the Birmingham of Our Grandsons*. It was published by the socially progressive Quaker chocolatiers Cadbury of Bournville in 1943. By that time many of the images in it must have been erased by the actions of the Luftwaffe, in preparation for the city council's own blitzkrieg. Its closing pages propose a prescriptive vision of Birmingham's utopian urban future:

> WHEN WE BUILD AGAIN WE MUST NOT REPEAT OUR OLD MISTAKES – No more congested streets. No more overcrowded schools. No more dingy courts. No more drab districts. No more huddled houses. BUT CREATE A CITY OF WHICH OUR GRANDCHILDREN WILL BE PROUD. With more green parks. With healthier houses. With sunny airy schoolrooms. With fine hospitals. With better factories. With good gardens.

An architect's impression of 'what a rebuilt Jewellery Quarter might look like' prefigures the arrival of the Bull Ring shopping centre of 1964, subsequently torn down in 2000 before it could be rehabilitated. Three of the sculptor Trewin Copplestone's four mighty primitive beaten-iron Bull Forms that adorned it are lost, presumed stolen or destroyed, Bamiyan bull Buddhas blown apart before the town planner Taliban.

In 1943, the Cadbury book says, the city still had 38,000 basic back-to-backs, and 100,000 tunnel-back homes. Being fortunate enough to work on the shop floor at Joseph Cadbury's chocolate factory, my grandparents frequented the landscaped environs of his experimentally idyllic Bournville village, where to this day there is not a public house in sight, and yet the consumption of chocolate remains compulsory.

My nan was laid off by the Quakers when she married in 1937, as they believed wives shouldn't work. The certificate, which I have a copy of, reads: 'The directors of Cadbury Brothers Limited desire to express their best wishes to Emma Burton on her leaving Bourneville and their appreciation of her fourteen years of loyal co-operations. For the directors, George Cadbury, Bournville, 3rd Septermber 1937.'

When the war decimated his male workforce, George Cadbury, a kind of chocolate pope with a hotline to heaven, reinterpreted God's will. Apparently the Almighty told Cadbury he would welcome all the women he'd laid off back to chocolate work, in the same way as he allowed colonies of frogs to spontaneously recalibrate their gender balance when required. Nothing was set in stone. The God of the chocolatiers was not a dictator.

My grandparents wanted to leave old dark Birmingham behind, but they were formed by it, and stained indelibly by it, and in their would-be upwardly mobile eyes this was a veritable Mark of Cain.

A man died mysteriously in my grandparents' road in 1973, and I remember my grandfather was interviewed about his deceased neighbour for ATV local news. I watched the report on TV, bewildered by the strange and strangled Lord Charles accent he felt obliged to put on for the cameras. My culturally-cowed grandfather, usually so sure of himself, was afraid of looking foolish, afraid of looking common, afraid of looking poor. So he struggled to bury his lovely Brummagem twang, which had effortlessly brought to life all the old Enoch and Ayli comedy routines, and the music hall songs he'd regularly recite to me as a boy.

In the Ape's Shadow

I 'ad a little donkey, I kep' 'im in the yard.
One day in the wintertime when it was snowing hard,
Mutha said the donkey would be cold out in the stall,
Bring 'im in the kitchen and let 'im have a warm.
'E came in and 'e bit me mother's ear,
Took it for a cabbage leaf and kicked the chandelier.
And out went the gas. When it was alight again
At me mother's ear the donkey 'ad a bite again.
Mother went to get a fork to stick it in the ass,
But stuck it into Father's 'ead and out went the gas.

My grandmother was one of nine sisters, though one sister, a family-tree-researching relative now suspects, may not have been a sister as such. My childhood seemed to comprise of endless trips with my mother – most of her cousins having emigrated or moved far away – to clear one aunt's former home after another.

The recently deceased old ladies, named for flowers and dead queens, departed after determined struggles against death on the wards of various Victorian hospitals, and left only trails of wartime newspaper and biscuit-tinned memories, under the beds of a succession of vertical graves, in Smethwick, Selly Oak and Kings Norton.

I sat by the brick backyard toilets of untended gardens and moved snails from step to step as personal effects were removed. And now I have inherited a photograph album my mother painstakingly assembled, of curled pictures of this extended sisterhood, captioned with her Medical Secretarial efficiency:

Auntie Elsie and mother at 31 Dad's Lane,
   Moseley, Burton family home.
1923 Mother at Raddlebarn Lane School,
   sitting first on right. School still in Selly
   Oak today.
Shirley Carnival, attendant to Carnival Queen.
Mother with the Shirley Singers.

I was four years old when, having moved in with my grandparents, I eventually started school at Streetsbrook Infants, just up from their house on Arnold Road. Richard Hammond, the accident-prone cultural provocateur from Amazon TV's *The Grand Tour*, was in the year below me, apparently, but I do not remember him.

Soon after our inconvenient arrival in his home, my grandfather had a stroke, from which he eventually made a good recovery, but I was required to move around the house, for what felt like years, with quietness and caution while he convalesced.

It was, I expect, a difficult mode of existence for a four-year-old boy, wrenched from the home he knew, and I remember everyone's angry disappointment when, for no good reason, I deliberately threw an important key into the brick square of the garden vegetable patch, where it was subsequently lost.

I felt trapped in a kind of limbo, wondering when we would return to 'our' house, a cosy and airy new-build box, with big windowpanes and white clapperboard, on the corner of a utilitarian green space in a sixties estate, where my father now waited out his legal wranglings, smoking and drinking, and eating pork chops and kidneys and boiled potatoes alone.

How sad and lonely my dad must have been, I now realise, years too late to do anything about it. But I wanted my toys back, probably, and our little garden, where once abundant urban hedgehogs came up to the windows to lick saucers of milk by moonlight, back before their numbers were decimated by whatever the fuck it is we're doing to this burning world.

My little friend Nigel from round the corner, who went on to join The King's Singers, told me he had kept coming round and knocking all through the years of my absence, but my dad told him I wasn't in.

When my father finally vacated the house in our favour, and we went back, after a few years at my grandparents', it seemed like the *Marie Celeste*. His favourite fish-faced glazed-green ashtray lay abandoned, and I still have it on the mantelpiece, even though I am now a non-smoker. Fag ends wilted within its gaping mouth, as if my father had left in a hurry, like someone fleeing the scene of a crime.

On an estate agent's website, where the house sold for £250,000 last year, I look at the photographs of the refitted interior and I can see the exact spot where the nest of tables, with that forgotten ashtray, stood. I mowed that lawn; those windows ran wet with melting pre-global-warming winter morning ice; in that bedroom, I tore my frenulum, and spurted a fountain of blood, in an incautious bout of dry-humping; that is the oak tree I climbed.

At the point we moved back in, unbeknownst to me, Nikki Sudden and Epic Soundtracks, aka Adrian & Kevin Godfrey, future founders of Birmingham's Sonic Youth-inspiring art punks the Swell Maps, were schoolboy T-Rex fans living in a large detached house with their parents on the corner of Ravenswood Drive and Widney Lane.

This address was not one minute's walk away, and I was later to deliver free weekly estate agents' sponsored newspapers to it. Sudden even attended the same secondary school as me, I learned, but a generation earlier.

I am aware that these facts have no meaning. I am aware that I am inserting myself into a Birmingham punk rock narrative that I am not part of. I wasn't interested in John Peel and Barbarella's in 1977. I read American Marvels from the newsagent's spinner, like *Deathlok the Demolisher*, *Howard the Duck*, *Werewolf by Night*, *Warlock* and *Captain Marvel*, and drew comics indoors like a nancy boy.

Earlier this year the lost 1977 demos of TV Eye, Birmingham's first garage punk band, were at last issued by Easy Action records. The inner sleeve shows the group performing on a park bandstand on a Saturday afternoon, watched only by still-flared children, their Chopper bikes abandoned, their hands sticky with the juice of space-rocket-shaped ice lollies and FABs.

One lone legitimate audience member – it could be Sudden himself in a Greek fisherman's cap, to be honest – watches TV Eye, leant against a table.

But I am not that lone audience member, however much I would like to have been. I would have been at my dad's Blossomfield Road flat that afternoon, on Access Day, eating toast, with blueberry jam he had stolen from a Dutch hotel breakfast buffet, while in Amsterdam, selling cardboard to Europe.

At the other end of my paper route from the Sudden/Soundtracks home, where the fringes of the Birmingham conurbation dissolved into the now ravaged green belt, Widney Lane headed towards the wilderness of rural Warwickshire and the now decimated Blythe Valley.

And there, at the point where the countryside dissolved, was a new housing estate. I learned, only last year, that it contained the final home of the poet and painter Emmy Bridgwater, who spent her last decades there before dying in 1999.

Born in Edgbaston and a member of the Birmingham Surrealist group in the thirties, and chosen for Paris's 1947 *Exposition Internationale du Surréalisme* by Andre Breton himself, the talented and striking Bridgwater abandoned her artistic endeavours in the late forties to care for her mother and disabled sister, stopping short of becoming the significant figure she might have been.

Emmy was also the woman for whom the Italian surrealist Toni del Renzio left his wife Ithell Colquhoun, whose recently republished travel writings I wrote introductions for, and whose unexpected autograph I suddenly found in a book of hers I had owned for years.

But above all her other noteworthy achievements, Bridgwater would also have been a weekly recipient of a copy of *Solihull Property Times*, delivered by the twelve-year-old me on foot, on Friday nights, between the end of school and the start of *The Tube* on Channel 4.

Bridgwater's late poem, 'Over', a pathetic fallacy written in 1982, near the end of our unwitting newspaper delivery relationship, describes a ruined landscape and concludes with the notion of water covering the land...

In floods so smooth that boats could ride above the grumbling ground
And never seen, neglected, covered over,
Earth forgotten or recalled
Remaining under the shining surface
Lost
It shall be lost there.

Birmingham Surrealists? Who would have dreamed there even were such things? Certainly not me, as a would-be surrealist teenager, and I would have wept with joy if I had known they existed, and then tried to track them down.

Either side of World War II, the Birmingham Surrealists met at the Kardomah Café on New Street, and planned their surreal Birmingham escapades, perhaps intending to place faggots on a telephone cradle, or fill Duchamp's urinal with the local custard, Bird's. Today their café clubhouse is a men's outfitters called Hawes and Curtis.

I went in there a few years ago, looking for traces of surrealism that I had overlooked as a youth. A smartly suited young Asian assistant approached me, with retail hair, and saw me in a kagoul so smelly my wife finally took it off me in the street and threw it into a public waste bin in a fit of shame.

'Can I help you, sir?'

I told him I was looking for the Surrealists' café, more to amuse myself than anything, knowing already that this trouser-vending dolt would know nothing of the Birmingham Surrealists. The boy proudly took me outside and showed me the Kardomah logo, still carved into the brickwork above, and I was ashamed of my assumptions.

I once recognised Nikki Sudden, around 1992, serving behind the counter of a collectors' record shop off Oxford Street in London. He would not be drawn on his Solihull schooldays, as it might no doubt have punctured his legend, offering me instead an unreleased 7" Cream acetate to smell, by way of compensation.

Adrian Godfrey, a Solihull schoolboy, had remade himself as Nikki Sudden. The patchwork of seventies heroin rock shapes that became his assumed persona was a far more significant work of art than most of the music he left behind, which was made fascinating mainly by the fabricated persona of its performer, rather than the quality of his songs themselves.

Sudden's solo discography is vast, but has the feel of a man who, when money was short, would dash into the nearest European studio to provide a record label run by a fan with some collateral to service a debt. It has to be cherry-picked judiciously.

Accept the apparently flawed package as an art experiment and it works. If this person – Adrian Godfrey – were to live as this other person – Nikki Sudden – how would his life have panned out? Having failed to become Keith Richards, this Sudden persona still had to live by Keith Richards' rules, even without the money and fame to make that lifestyle sustainable.

But all acts are constructs to an extent. When I started doing stand-up I viewed 1979's alternative comedy explosion as a punk era scorched-earth moment, before which all comedy was rubbish. Now I long to feel part of a continuum, and in the old variety theatres I sit in the dressing rooms and use Google on my laptop to work out which nineteenth-century comedians may have sat exactly where I sit now.

In the spring of 2016, I sat backstage at the Wolverhampton Grand, an 1894 variety palace with the kind of perfect acoustics and sightlines that Victorian theatre architects, in the shadow of Frank Matcham, seemed to nail every time with an accuracy that no longer seems achievable.

I discovered the dressing room was once occupied by the early twentieth-century music hall comedian Fred Barnes, an openly gay Birmingham-born act who was always accompanied by a marmoset that sat on his shoulder. Fred's 1907 sheet music smash 'The Black Sheep of the Family' was the LGBT anthem of its day, and is still sung by contemporary drag acts.

The tune debuted at The Hackney Empire, where I won the New Act of the Year competition eighty-three years later, and was handed an award inscribed to 'Steward Lee'. I supposed Fred and I both got our big breaks there. Suddenly a huge success, Fred quaffed the Black Sheep profits, and was eventually arrested while drunk-driving with a topless sailor, leading a judge to declare him 'a menace to His Majesty's Fighting Forces'.

Fred first got noticed in 1906, in *Cinderella* at the Alexandra Theatre in Birmingham, playing a character called, mockingly, the Duke of Solihull, a name I wish I had adopted, and may yet assume. But by the 1930s, he had retreated in an alcoholic haze to Southend-on-Sea, playing his hit in seafront pubs to anyone who remembered him, his extravagant marmoset replaced by a humble chicken. Fred committed suicide in 1938, far from the city of his birth, under that wrong and too-wide sky of south-east England.

Imagining Fred Barnes backstage at Wolverhampton Grand, probably drunk between shows, I suddenly felt very sad for him, and didn't want Birmingham's Black Sheep Boy to be forgotten. So I went immediately onto eBay and found a signed photo of Fred Barnes in his 1907 pomp, for £2, and it hangs to this day in our lavatory, just above the toilet roll dispenser. I think it's what Fred Barnes would have wanted.

Fred Barnes, the fibreglass monkey and I all left the city that shaped us. I think I did the best out of the decision. The ape was smashed. And so was Fred, repeatedly, ending his days in a double act with a chicken. I was still in one piece, and though I had briefly been in a double act, it was with a man called Richard Herring who, whatever his faults, was better than a chicken.

Of course Nikki Sudden couldn't talk to me about Adrian Godfrey's schooldays, from behind the record shop counter. The story would cease to make sense. But Sudden's autobiography, a curiously un-self-aware, but weirdly compelling, read called *The Last Bandit*, does detail his dealings with the same eccentric Solihull teachers whose war-damaged wits I also enjoyed.

'Green Shield Stamps', an acoustic ballad Sudden released on his final album in 2007, is a disturbingly detailed description of the exact psychogeography of my own childhood, pretty much down to the postcode, even mentioning my old form at school.

In the Ape's Shadow

Mum, she saved up all those Green Shield Stamps.
We'd go swimming down Tudor Grange baths,
Up to the lido on those hot summer days,
Ride our bikes up and down Widney Lane.

This evocation of my own adolescence sounds, typically of Sudden, as if it were a tossed-off seventies Rolling Stones out-take, but written by a man whose dangerous predilections the music industry had no vested interest in indulging. Sudden died alone in a New York hotel room in 2006, hours after coming home from a sparsely attended acoustic set. He was forty-nine.

I was introduced to Sudden's brother, the more talented but less acclaimed drummer and songwriter Epic Soundtracks, outside a pub in Camden in the early nineties, by a woman I vaguely knew, called Sabina. But Soundtracks died, under similar circumstances, a decade before his brother. My Australian indie rock hero Dave Graney, a friend and admirer of Epic Soundtracks' own epic songwriting and assiduously curated record collection, wrote 'A Boy Named Epic' about him.

A boy named Epic, took his own name from a big book.
It's funny how your life becomes a story that you thought you were writin'.

Doesn't everyone's life become a story they are writing? Did Nikki Sudden and Epic Soundtracks only make that truth more explicit by operating under unwieldy pseudonyms that eventually became their actual personalities nonetheless? Isn't that what I am doing here, creating a viable Genesis myth, instead of writing the ten thousand words on the Birmingham post-punk scene the publisher signed me up for?

I did not know Swell Maps as boys. I never knowingly met Emmy Bridgwater. I didn't even see The Nightingales, first time around, and I could have done, fuck it. If I had my adolescence again I would write my Birmingham story differently. In a parallel eighties, Emmy Bridgwater and I, the New Solihull Surrealists, get the train into Moor Street Station and take tea, Kardomah Café style, on the shop floor of Hawes and Curtis, whether the sock and trouser salespeople like it or not.

What a Birmingham that would have been. But it wasn't my Birmingham. It was a Birmingham I

In the Ape's Shadow

built subsequently, in my imagination, from bits of Birmingham I overlooked at the time, a cut and paste collage as untrue in its own way as the Frankenstein's Monster of Nikki Sudden's bohemian sub-Stones persona; my remembered Birmingham was an unsteady structure, set nonetheless on two solid foundation stones; the pub bombings, and that enormous ape, in Manzoni Gardens.

The statue was called 'King Kong' – tiny Nanetta Stocker's magical inversion – and I was allowed to stop and marvel at it every week on our way to secure Nan's endlessly deferred Spot the Ball jackpot. And it was the single most exciting thing I had ever seen, a brutal beast, transplanted from some fantastic jungle to the contrived garden construct of this city centre square.

Oh, to be that ape! To have that power. You don't have to be Sigmund Freud to work out the attraction of that vast figure to a fatherless four-year-old former orphan who wasn't even sure where he lived, dependent on the kindness of an elderly couple, his mother away working daytimes, and studying at night school in the evenings, with an eye on future prospects.

'Who was King Kong?' I asked my grandfather, who had previously and patiently explained the breakup of The Beatles to me, after their formal dissolution, by pointing at the montage of multiple passport-style photos on the sleeve of my mother's copy of 'A Hard Day's Night', which I still treasure to this day.

'Well,' he had said, 'he fell out with him and he fell out with him and he fell out with him and he fell out with him and he fell out with him and he fell out with him and he fell out with him and he fell out with him and he fell out with him and he fell out with him and he fell out with him and that was the end of The Beatles.'

'Who was King Kong? He was a big monkey,' my grandfather said, 'and they caught him and put him in a zoo but he didn't like it so he ran away and then they killed him.' Bearing in mind that it would have been forty years since he had seen the film, this wasn't a bad effort, especially by today's standards.

A summary of my last stand-up show on Netflix's own listings reads, 'Reports of sharks falling from the skies are on the rise again. And nobody on the Eastern Seaboard is safe.'

When I finally got to see the original 1933 King Kong, on late-night TV in the early eighties, I am sure some of my excitement was due to the early impact of that awe-inspiring statue, and my grandfather's terse précis.

In the Ape's Shadow

Indeed, to this day, when I watch the end of the movie, where Carl Denham stands over Kong's body and sums up what we have seen with the famous line, 'Oh, no, it wasn't the airplanes. It was Beauty killed the Beast,' in my mind the showman is turning to the press and saying, 'He was a big monkey, and they caught him and put him in a zoo but he didn't like it so he ran away and then they killed him.'

I know that we stopped seeing the statue in the square after a while, and my grandmother was unable to explain where it had gone. And I remember that in November 1974, having been rattled by the pub bombings, Nan finally decided to trust the postman with the Spot the Ball coupon, and she never really travelled into the city centre again, not even to see Father Christmas in the grotto at Lewis's.

I also remember, briefly, seeing the statue once more, every week or so, for a short while, after it was transplanted to the forecourt of a garage, now renamed the King Kong Car Company, on the Stratford Road. But despite my protestations whenever we drove past him I was never allowed to get out and admire Kong close up again.

And then King Kong was gone, from the square, from the garage, from Birmingham. 'He was a big monkey, and they caught him and made him advertise a garage in Birmingham, but he didn't like it so he ran away.' I hoped that wherever Kong was now, he was finally free. I never forgot King Kong, whose reign of terror over Birmingham loomed large in my childhood memories.

No one else seemed to remember him though. Indeed, the absence of the giant Kong statue from the collective consciousness was so pronounced that, during my twenties, I began to wonder if I had imagined him. Perhaps this great stone ape, transplanted from his wild homeland to the concrete and ordered Manzoni-Madin landscape of Birmingham, had been some kind of subconscious dream manifestation of my own outsider status, a mutant talking duck transplanted to a world he never made.

Whenever I met a Midlander of my own age in my new home of nineties London I would quiz them about Kong. No one remembered him. And as this was before the internet, I couldn't just google 'King Kong Birmingham' and have my sanity confirmed by a reassuring Wikipedia page. Finally, an actor from Birmingham, Jack Corcoran, became the first person I ever met who had even a vague recollection of the stone ape. But he couldn't claim to be certain.

Then, in the summer of 1997, I managed to convince the *Sunday Times* to allow me to interview the lost and notoriously incommunicative sixties psychedelic legend Roky Erickson, the missing monkey king of proto-psychedelia. The former frontman of Austin's acid rock avatars The 13th Floor Elevators was now prepared to communicate with the Murdoch press through the medium of his mother, by telephone to her home in Texas.

At the time I was homeless due to a failed near marriage, and I was sofa-surfing in a flat with no phone line or mobile coverage. As I had to make the call in the small hours due to the time difference, which still applied even to Roky Erickson, the Culture Section said I could sit up all night in the *Sunday Times* offices and ring Roky Erickson's mother from the newspaper editor John Witherow's phone.

I sat in Witherow's dim office, waiting for the sun to set on Roky Erickson, far away on the other side of the world. I looked at the books on Witherow's shelves. Amongst biographies of Hitler, guides to fine wines, and detailed studies of organised crime, one volume stood out: *Public Sculpture of Birmingham Including Sutton Coldfield*. George T. Noszlopy. 1997.

And the first thing I thought of, twenty-four years since I first saw him, was Kong. I flipped to the index, my heart racing. '*King Kong* (Monro).' I could not believe it. Kong had been real. Kong was real. And then, I read on, and my joy turned to ashes in my mouth. 'Destroyed, formerly Bull Ring *xx-xxi*. 170.'

I turned to page 170. There was a black and white photo of King Kong, exactly as I remembered him, arms aloft, open-mouthed, Madin's Birmingham Post and Mail building visible on the horizon behind him, over the wall of Manzoni's walled garden, mounted on the concrete plinth where a little boy stood and admired him just as I had stood and admired him. I may not have been the capped observer at TV Eye's bandstand show or exchanged Christmas cards with Emmy Bridgwater, but that little Birmingham boy was me, as near as damn it. I read the entry.

King Kong

Nicholas Monro

1972
Reinforced coloured fiberglass
550cm high

In the Ape's Shadow

This sculpture was commissioned in 1972 by the Peter Stuyvesant Foundation for the City Sculpture project organised in collaboration with the Arts Council of Great Britain. Although it has long been absent from Birmingham, the massive fiberglass King Kong lives on in the memory of it citizens, as is evidenced by...

Apparently, the City Sculpture Project had instigated the creation of fourteen works which had a relationship to the various urban sites around the UK in which they were shown. Who was this Nick Monro genius, I wondered, whose fibreglass, and not stone apparently, ape seemed so in sync with the landscape around him?

Manzoni and Madin were trying to tame the wilds of Birmingham with the utilitarian concrete structures that Kong sat within, yet the giant ape's power showed us that nature was always waiting in the wings. Natural forms spiral alive on the rock Isaac Newton sits upon in Blake's famous etching. The mathematician tries to tame the universe while life teems unnoticed beneath his buttocks. Manzoni and

Madin would be forgotten. But this Blakean ape-spirit of the wildness of the world would survive.

Except it didn't. Birmingham City Council didn't pick up their option to purchase the figure, which was only in situ for six months (although those weekly visits to pay homage to it with my nan seemed, in my childhood memories, to last for years). The public didn't take the statue to their hearts, and many Brummies actively hated it.

As recently as last summer I found a post on a Birmingham history forum decrying Monro's monument. 'What I objected to in the Manzoni Gardens was the statue of King Kong,' wrote one David Grain, 'I regarded it as an insult to Sir Herbert Manzoni, a man I had met.'

And so, having insulted the late Sir Herbert Manzoni with his monkey presence, and after a brief tenure pimping his hairy ass for the King Kong car dealership like an ape whore, King Kong was eventually sold to Ingliston Public Market in Edinburgh, 'from where', wrote George T. Noszlopy in *Public Sculpture of Birmingham Including Sutton Coldfield*, 'it was eventually taken and destroyed'.

No fighter plane fight, no leading lady, and no majestic slow-motion skyscraper fall for this mighty

Kong, who battled the sun-blocking shapes of Manzoni's and Madin's concrete monsters daily, and won. Just the creeping death of civic indifference.

I was relieved that my memories were real, but distraught that having found Kong again on a shelf in John Witherow's office, I then discovered within seconds that I had missed my last chance to make his acquaintance one final time. Kong had slipped beyond me, through time, like Sudden and Soundtracks, and TV Eye and Emmy Bridgwater, fellow travellers from my childhood, but riding in carriages I never thought to enter.

I wish I could have saved King Kong. 'He was a big monkey, and they caught him and put him in a Scottish Market but he didn't like it so he ran away and then they killed him.'

Composing myself, I rang Roky Erickson's mother from John Witherow's phone. With a history of mental health issues that had left him a recluse, no one had ever expected Roky to record and perform again. But Craig Stewart, of Roky's new label Emperor Jones Records, said, 'Who am I to tell a fifty-two-year-old man that he can't sleep and watch TV all day? Sanest man in the world, if you ask me.

His mom says he's only as crazy as he wants to be, and I believe it.'

I wondered if, in a similar frame of mind, sick of the meddling world, maybe Nick Monro's King Kong had faked his own disappearance. Perhaps he made it north, fording the Firth of Forth, and was in the Highlands now, foraging and thriving, in a mountain-top bower of Scots pine and soft mosses, playfighting the Loch Ness Monster and rolling in cool Cairngorm snow.

Nineteen years later the promoters of the All Tomorrow's Parties festival booked Roky, who at seventy-one and on different medication was finally touring again, for a weekend in a north Wales holiday camp that I had been invited to program. His tour bus arrived a night earlier than expected, before the festival had started. The name Roky Erickson meant nothing to the regular holiday camp security guard at Pontin's Prestatyn, so Roky's entourage were forced to pitch up on the promenade. Relations between band and promoters rapidly deteriorated. I kept out of the way. They say you shouldn't meet your heroes. And I didn't, sadly.

Last Wednesday night, the 22 of June, was the last night of the first leg of my current tour. We were in Wolverhampton, and after the show I went to the Wetherspoons opposite the theatre with another one of my heroes, Robert Lloyd of Birmingham's invincible post-punks The Nightingales, who I have met, repeatedly. And it's been fine. Rob is like someone I would have known anyway, and didn't, but do now.

There's a distinctive strain of post-war working-class bohemians whose ilk have been legislated out of existence by successive Tory governments, never to be seen again. Robert Lloyd has survived decades outside the system, wheeling and dealing in fertile cracks, and continues to produce exceptional work in conjunction with a supportive cast of musicians, even after a stroke briefly felled this great oak of a man a few years back.

On this tour, I've psyched myself up before shows playing Robert's 2006 song 'Born Again in Birmingham', a krautrockabilly rumble shredded with spiky shards of social observation, through the theatre PAs. I think the lyrics are a cynical description of a certain kind of muck and brass Birmingham businessman, though I worry about interpreting Lloyd, one of our great unsung rock poets. I once spoke admiringly of his use of a bakery, in 'Use Your Loaf', as a metaphor for society. 'What are you talking about?' he answered, 'I worked in a bakery when I left school. It's just about that.'

I had arranged to meet Robert, and an entourage drawn from the current line-up of The Nightingales and the nineties Birmingham radiophonic band Pram, after a performance at the beautiful Wolverhampton Grand. Unlike his fellow Brummie Fred Barnes, The Duke of Solihull, Robert Lloyd never had a hit, though his band The Nightingales recorded more John Peel sessions than any other act, even the tastemaker's beloved Fall.

In 1990, at the end of one incarnation of The Nightingales and before the implementation of the next, Lloyd even made a polished solo album of quirky but ignored art pop for a major label, augmented by big name session musicians, which in retrospect seems to prefigure the national treasure template that Jarvis Cocker subsequently came, by a different route, to inhabit.

Though The Nightingales have, somehow, never enjoyed the kind of critical rehabilitation that has retrospectively canonised contemporaries like Wire, Mission of Burma or Gang of Four, when Lloyd reconvened the group after a fifteen-year layoff in 2004 it was as a going concern, not as a vaudeville punk nostalgia act.

He could have reformed The Prefects, his first group, and traded their Clash White Riot tour credentials in for short-term commercial gain, but he instead chose the hard graft of starting again from scratch.

When I met Robert for our annual Wolverhampton post-show drink I found myself not so much talking to him, as grilling him about the Birmingham punk scene that spawned his band, like some kind of gauche eighties fanzine editor. I think the proposed subject of this piece was still percolating in my brain, and I reverted to gentleman amateur journalist mode. But Robert Lloyd isn't interested in the past.

Why did Birmingham's post-punk scene not enjoy the sense of identity that coalesced in Manchester, around Factory Records, or in Liverpool, around Eric's and the Teardrops/Bunnymen/Wah! axis? How was Andy Wickett, of Birmingham's TV Eye, compensated for surrendering the riff of 'Stevie's Radio Station' to Duran Duran that went on to underpin their big hit, 'Girls on Film'?

Did Robert remember short-lived Birmingham sensations like The Denizens, or Dangerous Girls, bands who never even made albums, their cult status built on stand-out singles like 'Ammonia Subway' and the eponymous 'Dangerous Girls' respectively?

Lloyd dismissed everyone I mentioned as middle-class dilettantes, and it's easy to see why. He's the last man standing, still moving forward, his best work still perhaps ahead of him, playing flat out seventy-minute stream-of-consciousness sets with no breaks between the songs, powered by whisky and self-belief, an unlikely but still impossibly compelling frontman in sensible suit, spectacles and shirt. He is our greatest still unassimilated alt-rock talent.

The Denizens Robert doesn't remember, though he may have met them. Dangerous Girls got to play everywhere because they had a PA, he says, and pubs didn't have their own in those days. He's not interested in what I think his early contemporaries could have been, or what they mean in retrospect to someone who wasn't there, and he's not interested in nostalgia. Lloyd's still looking to the future, his head full of the usual fabulous dreams and schemes, and does anyone here tonight have a bottle of whisky back at their flat for when Wetherspoons call time.

Between pints Robert explains, 'The best three Birmingham bands, from the modern age, by which I mean after Black Sabbath and all that, are us, UB40 and the City of Birmingham Symphony Orchestra. I wrote to the bloke from the CBSO and told him that, told him we should do a Christmas single, an Elvis cover, The Nightingales and The City of Birmingham Symphony Orchestra, because we're both the best at what we do. I sent him all these reviews saying we're brilliant, meet him halfway, you know. He had me in to see him, the bloke, but the thing is you have to plan so far ahead with these orchestras, they have so many commitments.'

Mad as it sounds, were it to happen, this cross-cultural collaboration would be massive and, if you've ever heard one of Robert's more sensitive songs, you'll know he has the Elvis in Vegas voice to pull it off. For a moment I find myself mentally calculating how one would go about realising this strange project, and then look at the empty pints and shot glasses around me in the bright Wednesday night Wetherspoons light and realise I'm probably not thinking straight.

By the end of the evening, at some bizarre karaoke/open-mic club on a cobbled Wolverhampton side street, after Rob has told me about the time he walked in on Bo Diddley in his underpants, when trying to steal booze from his Brixton Academy dressing room, and his drummer Fliss has damaged us all with an unnamed spirit, I feel I am starting to irritate my elders.

I am, after all, still an annoying fan, and probably one of those middle-class dilettantes too, I think, ruining proper jokes with skills learned from an English degree, wrung from an undeserved opportunity, procured in part through an educational grant reserved for 'waifs and strays'.

Stand-up wasn't the only thing I could have done. I should probably have been a teacher, doing some good in the world. For Robert Lloyd, kicked out at sixteen from the grammar school he was somehow bounced up into, rock and roll was the only route out of the Birmingham bakery, 'where the flunkies dated packers, the bosses got to date creamers, and the jokes were handed down like diseases'.

> *I learned all three, threw them away*
> *But I remember them even today.*
> *"I only work here for the bread",*
> *"I need the dough",*
> *"Use your loaf."*

('Use Your Loaf', 1982)

In the Ape's Shadow

The Birmingham Kong was wrecked. Robert Lloyd is still defiant and roaring. I, in contrast, I must admit, am flagging a little.

I can't thread myself back into the Birmingham I'd like to have been a part of. I am happy to know Robert Lloyd now, as a forty-nine-year-old adult, but I think I'd have been just an annoying hanger-on had we been contemporaries in the eighties Birmingham subculture of my imagination.

So many great comedians, with better minds than mine, who were my initial contemporaries, disappeared and gave up, without even a YouTube camera-phone clip to show for their years of persistence. But I'm the equivalent of the late seventies Birmingham punk scene second-stringers who ended up in Duran Duran, striking it rich while greater talents starved.

Nikki Sudden, for example, my childhood near-neighbour, had a sense of vocal pitch which, though extremely poor, was not quite as unreliable as that of the millionaire playboy yachtsman Simon Le Bon, and yet he faded away alone in a New York hotel room.

That said, Sudden's boastful autobiography is at pains to point out that, despite his lack of money or acclaim, he still slept with no end of aristocratic supermodels. And stole their stash. At the point of his death, I wonder, did he turn back into Adrian Godfrey, Solihull schoolboy, or was it Nikki Sudden, in his peacock scarves and Stones cast-off French Revolution finery, who went to meet his maker?

For the sake of creating the illusion of structure, there's an important part of this largely incoherent narrative which, having discovered, I held back to the end for dramatic effect.

A few years after I finally got online, around the turn of the new century, it finally occurred to me to check for information about the Birmingham King Kong. I accepted that the statue had been destroyed, as detailed in George T. Noszlopy's *Public Sculpture of Birmingham Including Sutton Coldfield*, but wondered if there was anyone out there with fond memories of the work.

Initially all I found was contemporary local news footage of pinch-faced Brummies interviewed in Manzoni Gardens, hating the monstrosity, and condemning it as a waste of public money. And the sculptor Nicholas Monro, it turned out, was a pop artist who explored the power of iconic images. He must have known exactly what he was doing when he positioned Kong in that warren of concrete, amidst those mithering people.

And then, as I dug deeper, it turned out Noszlopy was wrong. Rumours of the Birmingham King Kong's death, like those of the Birmingham folk fiddler Dave Swarbrick's in 1999, had been greatly exaggerated. Kong wasn't destroyed in the Edinburgh market in the late seventies, though he did endure terrible suffering, painted pink, and then in a tartan pattern, and finally having his arm smashed off by Scottish hooligans. Even in statue form Kong played out the same humiliations at the hands of senseless humans as he did in the mythic movie that inspired Munro's sculpture.

In 2005 the damaged statue was moved by the market's owner, one Nigel Maby of the Spook Erection company, to his outdoor auction site in Penrith, where it was left lying on its back in a car park. After Nigel's death, Kong was finally put out to grass, prostrate once more, in the moorland garden of Maby's widow, Lesley, where he lay, staring upwards at the scudding clouds.

In the summer of 2016 I took the kids to an exhibition at Somerset House on the Strand about lost public sculpture of the sixties and seventies. The narrative of the show suggested that a great period in public art had ended, and that pieces meant to stimulate passers-by into thinking differently about their environment had been callously treated, and even abandoned and lost, by the officials that inherited them.

Monro's King Kong was not present, but a series of panels told Kong's story. Once more I was moved to tears, and the kids were as bewildered as they always are by my inexplicable displays of emotion. They will remember me, as adults, crying at inanimate objects and weeping at abstract sounds.

In the spring of 2017, Kong was lifted onto a flatbed truck from Lesley Maby's garden and driven to Leeds, where, fully rehabilitated, he became the centrepiece of a retrospective exhibition at The Henry Moore Institute, commemorating all the entries in that 1972 City Sculpture Projects scheme.

Maybe it was judicious editing, but news footage showed that passers-by in Leeds who saw him mounted at the Institute's doorway could find nothing but kind things to say about him. A bearded man of about my age remembered being taken to see him in Birmingham by his parents, and was clearly delighted to encounter King Kong again.

In the Ape's Shadow

Now there are calls for the city of Birmingham to buy King Kong back, doubtless at a far greater price than they were first offered him in 1973. Personally, I don't know if Birmingham can be trusted with Kong. It has lost three of Trewin Copplestone's Bull Forms, that once adorned the Bull Ring; William Bloye's 1958 statue of the city's Industrial Revolution powerhouses Boulton, Watt and Murdoch, has recently been re-gilded so gaudily that it looks more like a window display in the Rackhams department store than a dignified memorial to the city's innate inventiveness; and Bloye's protégé Raymond Mason (OBE)'s 1991 fibreglass celebration of the city's history, *Forward*, was literally melted into nothing by arsonists in 2003. There's something about the city and its sculptures.

But returning to modern Birmingham in triumph, Kong would find the concrete circus that previously imprisoned him erased from history. In this version of the King Kong legend, Kong escapes and outwits his captors, only to see the apparatus of his torment obliterated. And I think Kong would seem even more powerful and immortal in Birmingham now, presiding over the ephemera of that bulbous silver Selfridges and the wiry hatchings of the new library, than he did against the monumental, if flawed, edifices of Manzoni and Madin.

The Birmingham that King Kong left is no more. But he was formed in complementary opposition to it, and has carried its influence with him, surveying the vast sweep of its post-war history, whilst painted pink and then tartan and then deformed in Edinburgh, then flat on his great broad back in the green grass of the Lake District, and finally triumphant once more in a Leeds city square. He would not be as he is, had he not been raised in the city. Wherever he comes to rest, Birmingham is within him.

HOMETOWN TALES

HOMETOWN TALES: BIRMINGHAM
Original Tales by Regional Writers
MARIA WHATTON
STEWART LEE

HOMETOWN TALES: GLASGOW
Original Tales by Regional Writers
KIRSTY LOGAN
PAUL MCQUADE

HOMETOWN TALES: HIGHLANDS & HEBRIDES
Original Tales by Regional Writers
COLIN MACINTYRE
ELLEN MACASKILL

HOMETOWN TALES: LANCASHIRE
Original Tales by Regional Writers
JENN ASHWORTH
BENJAMIN WEBSTER

AVAILABLE NOW FROM W&N

Original Tales by Regional Writers

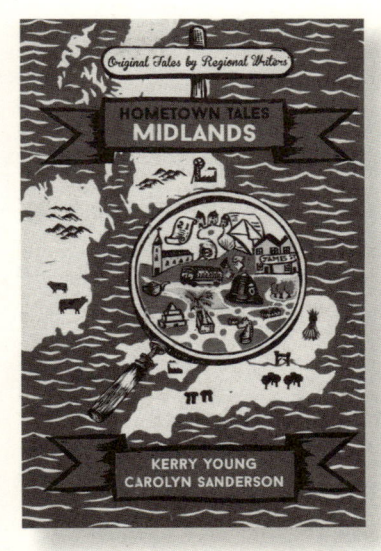

HOMETOWN TALES: MIDLANDS
KERRY YOUNG
CAROLYN SANDERSON

HOMETOWN TALES: SOUTH COAST
GEMMA CAIRNEY
JUDY UPTON

HOMETOWN TALES: WALES
TYLER KEEVIL
ELUNED GRAMICH

HOMETOWN TALES: YORKSHIRE
CATHY RENTZENBRINK
VICTORIA HENNISON

AVAILABLE NOW FROM W&N

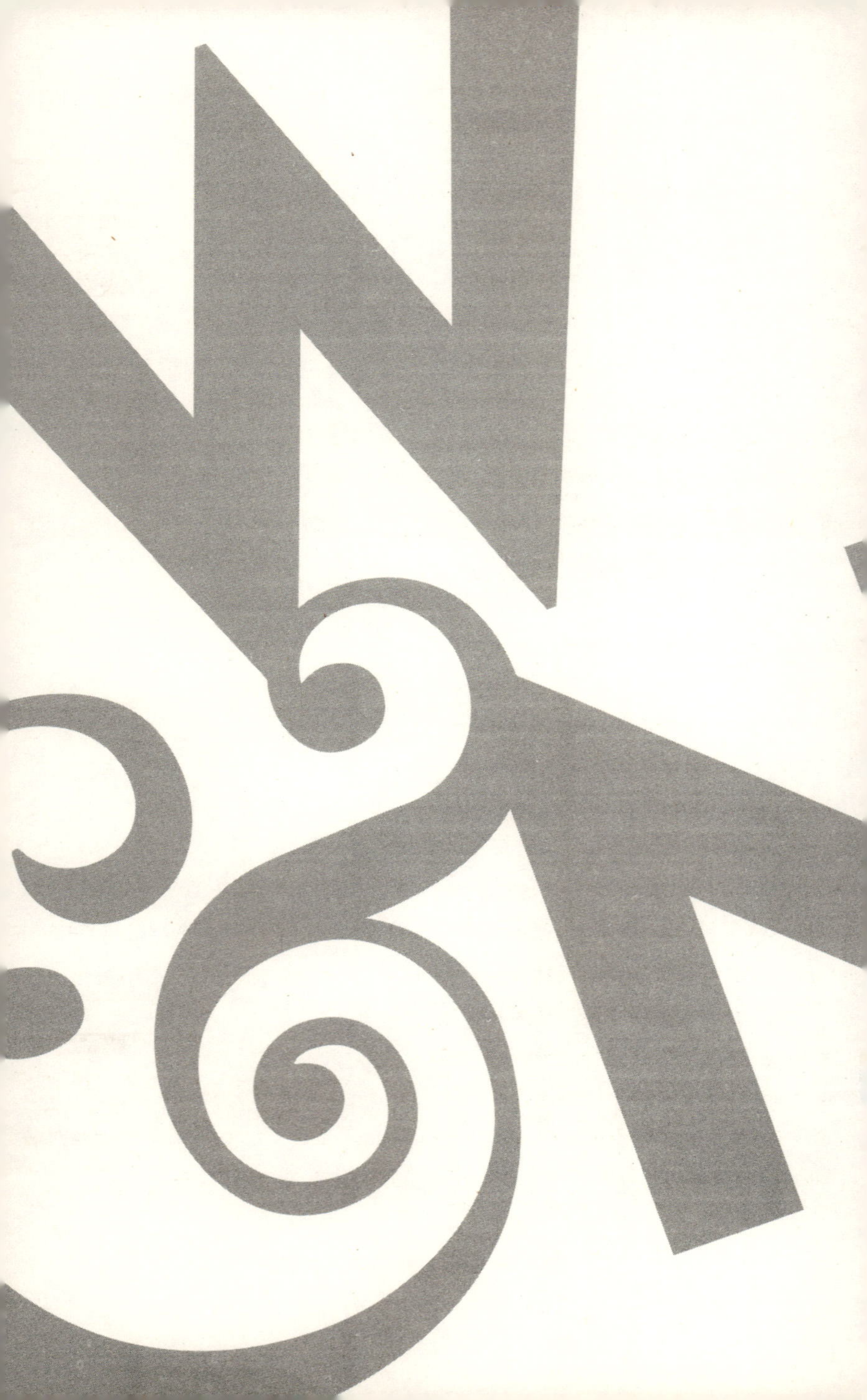